THE RULES OF FUNDRAISING

Douglas K. Shaw

CEDAR
RIVER
MEDIA

Doug Shaw is among a very small handful of the most out-standing direct response fundraisers in the country. His firm is one of the largest and most effective.

Now he has a book that exposes us to all his years of experience and expertise. It's an amazing book.

Doug claims he doesn't believe in rules. Then he gives us 35 rules that are profound and inviolate. It's like opening up a treasure chest.

This book is replete with stories of the great and near-great. You get to know what has worked and what hasn't. And you get to know a great deal about Doug and what makes him tick.

You don't have to be in direct mail to prize this volume. Doug has made a valuable contribution to the field and our profession. This book is a must. Get one for your desk, for quick reference, and for your library.

JEROLD PANAS
Executive Partner — Jerold Panas, Linzy & Partners

TABLE OF CONTENTS

INTRODUCTION

I'm a person who grew up on the wrong side of the tracks. There were six of us living south of Seattle in a little shack made out of Boeing Aircraft Company packing crates. I know our house was used to ship airplane parts because it was stenciled in large black letters all over the outside. Not a thing you want the kids in your neighborhood to notice, "Hey, you wanna play ball with that kid that lives in the box?"

As kids, my three sisters and I knew we didn't have much money but because it was the only world we knew, we had no context for understanding how desperately poor we really were. Oh, my dad would sometimes make comments about his own upbringing that were meant to make us feel fortunate to have a roof over our heads. One of his more repeatable and memorable lines was, "When I was growing up I was so poor I couldn't pay attention."

So my formative years were times that might have seemed normal in the days of the pioneers; we built our own little place to live, at first there was no electricity and running water meant getting a bucket and running outside to the cistern to get it. The outhouse was just far enough out back of the cabin to be supposedly sanitary (can any outhouse really be sanitary?) and certainly very inconvenient and scary in the dark, rain and snow. My mother cooked dinner on a Coleman gas stove, and the lantern rested on the kitchen table making its hissing sounds as the air we pumped into it forced the white gas up into the cloth of the hot, glowing mantle.

We basically lived a life of subsistence among other people who must have been curious, amazed or concerned at our standard of living. I was certain we were the family that people talked about, saying things like, "There goes the neighborhood!" especially on the day my dad decided to cut his old turtleback Chrysler sedan in half with a hacksaw.

He needed a pickup truck for his trade, bricklaying, but he couldn't afford to buy one, so he just chopped the car off right behind the driver's seat and built a plywood platform to carry his tools, bricks and mortar. Of course he did it in the driveway in full view of all the property owners on our street.

Most of our neighbors were just ordinary, hardworking people. Many of them worked for the company for which our house was stenciled, Boeing. They had small two-bedroom houses, cut their grass on Saturday and watered the gravel road in front of their homes to keep the dust down.

Speaking of dust, my dad, his parents and his nine siblings were part of the great migration that took place during what he called "the hungry thirties." They moved from a rock- infested Missouri dry farm to the Seattle area to escape the poverty of the dust bowl. To my young mind the gravel road in front of our house seemed like they just brought it with them.

We only aspired to be considered working class. In fact, we were just glad when my dad, with his third-grade education and a trade, had work of any kind.

With my beginnings I still find it pretty amazing that I was
able to graduate from high school, college and even graduate school. It wasn't until college, after many evenings of hanging out with friends and hearing their life stories, that I began to realize just how poor we really were.

I haven't written about my early years because I seek sympathy. In fact, most of the world has a more desperate existence than what I experienced as a child. Rather, my reason for telling you of my beginnings is to impress upon you that even though, at the time of writing, our country is in fiscal flux, and our elected officials seem to have lost their way, this is still very much the land of tremendous opportunity. Just ask any immigrant cab driver, landscaper or housekeeper, and they'll tell you how good we have it here in North America.

It was experiencing the powerlessness of poverty, firsthand, that led me to work at World Relief, a Christian relief and development organization. It was there that I was able to travel to far off places where entire families spent their whole lives scavenging the landfills of major cities like Manila or Mumbai. Later my journey would take me into the streets of the U.S. and Canada, where homeless and addicted men and women had lost all hope. My faith has grown as I've seen the lives of millions of people directly impacted by the generosity of God's people and the expertise of the great organizations and ministries our company has served.

For more than 45 years now I've had the privilege of participating in fundraising for Christian organizations. My apprenticeship began right out of seminary. It was a fulfilling and exhilarating experience to help provide food, clothing, shelter, medical assistance, self-sustaining work and Christian hope to hundreds of thousands of the world's most destitute people. My inspiring international experiences led to a burning desire to see more people engaged in this life-changing work by becoming donors. When a fundraising position opened up where I worked, I decided, with the encouragement of a colleague, to throw my hat in the ring. My life has never been the same.

Today I have the privilege of serving as Chairman of the Board/CEO of Douglas Shaw & Associates. We're a for-profit fundraising consulting firm of scores of very talented individuals who innovate, strategize, create and produce a vast array of fundraising and communications services for nonprofit organizations. It's through close association with my colleagues that I am able to present these Rules of Fundraising to you.

I have to confess though, it's a little difficult for a guy like me to try and tell anybody about the "rules" of anything. Mrs. Roberts, my third-grade teacher, would vouch for this, if she were still alive. Back then I hated rules. But as I've grown older, I've realized that rules can be gifts. And my hope for you is that you will see the Rules of Fundraising for what they really are: a helpful set of tools to encourage you, clear the path ahead of you and give you a craftsman's confidence as you use them to serve in this great effort of philanthropic encouragement.

These rules are being submitted to you as this old fundraiser's way of giving back to a community of dedicated, caring women and men who often work unnoticed, changing the world one life at a time.

It's written for development officers who need an old friend to turn to for expertise as they begin their journey, or to reorient the veteran fundraiser who wants to take the next step in his/her professional growth.

This book is also written for presidents or executive directors who need a road map for leading their development staff and to learn how important their leadership is in securing funding for the organization they lead.

It's also written for board members who know there must be some kind of fundraising best practices somewhere out there. It's a place they can turn to in order to serve their cause with greater knowledge and to make well-informed decisions about guiding the development efforts of the cause they've volunteered to serve.

My hope is that you will use this book as a reality check, as a kind of road map to help strengthen you on your journey. After all, it's all too easy to become entangled in the terminology, politics and culture of your own nonprofit and perhaps lose sight of the well-worn path where others have gone before. I'm so glad to share with you The Rules, which are one traveler's gift to another, with stories and examples to help you get to where you feel the road is calling you.

RULE #1

"There are rules in fundraising."

There are rules in fundraising, just like there are in quantum physics or any other field of study. Granted, these rules are not as complicated and involve a fairly low level of mathematical ability or else I'd be searching on LinkedIn for another job.

Let me be clear, following the rules won't guarantee success, but NOT following them will likely lead you to a much longer learning curve and quite possibly...failure.

To enable you to shorten your learning curve, try to visualize five or six veteran fundraisers sitting in the coffee shop of some hotel where a conference is being held. By now, most of them have been consultants for many years.

One of them is telling a story about a recent exchange with a client. That's what consultants do when they get together, they talk shop. The story being told is all too familiar. All the members of the group have been in this story themselves. They know the problem being described, and they know just how it's going to end. Experience is a great teacher, and all of them have a great deal of it. But it's not just experience that allows them to know how the story is going to end. All of them know there are specific inviolate rules in successful fundraising. The story they're listening to has revealed the breaking of at least one of the rules. So the story has to end badly.

Until now, no one I know has taken the time to write down the Rules of Fundraising; or perhaps they haven't wanted to expose these secrets or rules, fearing it might render their own knowledge less valuable. But as I see it, the rules existed long before I encountered them, and they'll be around long after I am gone, so let's see if we can do some good along the way. I must quickly add, however, this is not a comprehensive listing of the Rules of Fundraising; they're only the rules I have been able to gather from colleagues or learn by making my own mistakes thus far.

I spent many of my early years living on farms and ranches in the West and Midwest. Most of the houses we lived in had indoor plumbing, but several of them did not. Since rural living was so much a part of my formative years,

I'm afraid it made a greater impression on my young mind than I would have liked. My life was filled with chicken co-ops, cow pastures and barnyards, so I hope my earthy metaphors and stories serve to illustrate the existence and nuances of the rules rather than offend.

So let me get back to the rules. Now, I know they exist because, just like cow patties, every time I misstep it leaves me scraping my shoe. So, how can I help you to avoid this liquid languish? Bear with me; I promise there's hope coming.

I think it was pretty early in my illustrious career that I realized fundraising is different from the other "professions." There is no standardized governing or accrediting body specifically tasked with training or evaluating the experience and competency of individual fundraisers. The Evangelical Council for Financial Accountability (ECFA) sets, monitors and reports on ministry efficiency but not the effectiveness of individuals. The legal profession has the bar exam, and medical schools have their boards, and accounting has its Generally Accepted Accounting Practices (GAAP), but philanthropy is largely a self-governed, self-evaluating community. There is the Certified Fundraising Executive (CFRE) and more recently the Credentialed Christian Nonprofit Leader (CCNL) certifications, and they take a significant step toward measuring the body of knowledge mastered by fundraisers, but this book is about behavior rather than knowledge. It's about what works. It's about the rules that govern the successful raising of money for the cause you so dearly love.

RULE #2

"Nobody knows all the rules... including old guys like me."

When I first began raising funds, what seems like 200 years ago, I did well to find my way to my desk and the copier. We didn't have computers or e-mail yet, there was nothing like FedEx or even fax machines. I think we had a telex, you know the kind of loud pounding equipment that you always see in World War II movies? Thankfully Gutenberg had invented the printing press by this time, so we did have books, and I read everything I could get my hands on. Mostly, I was left to reading direct response tomes written by what I imagined to be funny little guys in glasses and bow ties sitting at the end of the hall in commercial advertising agencies. Even then, in 1980, Madison Avenue was just beginning to believe in direct response as a legitimate channel for communication and sales; the largest single substantiating fact being that it was an entirely measurable form of advertising, and the best thing was, you could determine the effectiveness of a campaign within weeks!

Commercial direct response guys like Richard Hodgson and Bob Stone no longer had to wait for the Arbitron or Nielsen ratings to tell them their market share. They could create their own market share by the use of direct mail, coupons, newspaper inserts, flyers or door hangers. And then came Ron Popeil, the famous TV infomercial pitchman, who launched the revolutionizing Pocket Fisherman and was later replaced as the on-air infomercial guru by the late Billy Mays!

In the 1980s, fundraising executives were just discovering that blue Sharpie underlining and the bolding of text in direct mail letters made a positive difference in their response. So they marked up everything, including each other I imagine, in blue underlining and giant parentheses until they discovered their next magic bullet—personalization! It was with great joy that they tested the use of mailing labels against addressing with dot matrix printers that could actually print directly on direct mail envelopes! Ah, it was a glorious time; the search for more magic bullets was on.

Fortunes were made by enterprising consultants as they offered up their next big thing.

During this same time, in the world of philanthropy, there was the beginning of a quiet movement taking shape.

In some cases it was forming within the ranks of non-profit organizations or ministries; the fledgling for-profit fundraising agencies serving nonprofits also made signifi-cant contributions to this effort. This grassroots migration came in the form of discovering principles vs. tactics. I've chosen, here, to call them The Rules, which goes against my aversion to authority but still seems to be the best way to articulate the unbroken truth of the principles that produce the greatest net income for nonprofits.

People like fundraising pioneer Claude Grizzard; crea-tive thought leader Maggie Haggberg; innovator Jerry Huntsinger; creative and strategic icon Jim Killion; major-gift author and guru Jerry Panas; pioneer and agency founder Russ Reid; brilliant strategist and friend Wiley Stinnett; major-gift strategist, mentor, teacher and author Bill Sturtevant; conservative political fundraiser Richard Viguerie; and prolific direct response mentor and consult-ant Mal Warwick, emerged as the practitioners of proven principles in fundraising. There are several others not mentioned here, not by intended exclusion but, perhaps, rather by my lack of knowledge, unconscious jealousy...or possibly plain petty disrespect.

I have personally had the honor of knowing most of these folks, worked directly with several of them and learned from them all. They each have their own areas of strength, but in general they have contributed greatly to the advancement of philanthropy by their discovery and use of the Rules of Fundraising.

It's difficult to find people inside or outside the non-profit world who have knowledge of most of the rules. Many people believe that their background in marketing or business qualifies them to serve as fundraisers; a great number of them have discovered that is rarely the case. Fundraising has its own rules, and most marketing folks find themselves struggling until they discover this ego-bruising truth. Unfortunately it's the nonprofit that has to suffer until the marketing professional comes to realize the truth. **A word to the board member or CEO of a non-profit, marketing experience does not equal fundraising experience.** Of course the reverse is true as well. Most seasoned fundraisers will tell you that there are overlaps between the disciplines of marketing and fundraising, but not enough to qualify a marketing person as a fundraiser. My most positive experiences with marketing people coming into the world of philanthropy is when the marketing professional recognizes the truth of this early on and simply says, "I'm from marketing, not fundraising. I have a lot to learn; will you teach me?"

The challenges in fundraising are great, and it requires years of experience and testing to begin to become skilled. John Gierach, the poet laureate of fly-fishing, once responded to a novice fly fisher's question, "Does it take very long to learn how to fly-fish?" with the hard truth statement, "It takes 10 years…if you fly-fish every day."

Even after a lifetime of direct response fundraising, any honest craftsman will tell you, they don't know it all. Nobody knows ALL the Rules of Fundraising, but this old guy can tell you, you have to start somewhere. We all did. Admitting to yourself that you don't know much is truthful and believable. It's probably most important that you can admit this to yourself. This is a character-forming insight that can free you up to become curious and humble, two traits that can help you greatly as you seek knowledge from those who have traveled the trail a little longer than you. Even old guys like me have mentors, and I count them as personal gifts to the spirit.

RULE #3

"Neither you nor I get to make the rules."

An extremely frustrating fact is neither you nor I get to make the rules. Like gold, all we can do is be relentless in seeking to discover the Rules of Fundraising. It requires a lot of pickaxe work, shoveling and back-breaking labor to amass enough rules to learn the difference between real gold and fool's gold. The veteran fundraiser will recognize the truth of this since they have done the work, carefully sifted through the soil and spotted the shiny nuggets amongst the stones along the banks of The River of Opportunity. That's why I've written this book. It's kind of a starter set of rules, if you will, to get you going on your own pilgrimage.

Again, we don't get to make the rules, they just exist! "So," you might ask, "if the rules aren't written down and few people can tell me what they are, how do I know they exist?" If the words, "Trust me" don't satisfy you, you may want to keep reading!

As a person committed to learning the fine art of fly-fishing for trout, I'm always in search of cold flowing streams. Some of the most famous trout rivers in North America are found in or near mountains where the melting snow runs off into the valleys to create rivers and streams. Just as cold water is necessary for the survival of trout, it's essential to know the rules to be an effective fundraiser. Now, for me, there's always excitement in finding a new place to throw in a line. Finding a new fundraising rule can, in many ways, produce a similar sense of discovery.

I wish I could create mountains! I truly do!

Living for in Illinois for many years, we had what I would consider a serious shortage of them. If you were to look online for trout fishing in Illinois, as I have, you'd see that it says, "See Wisconsin!" I'm not kidding here; it really says that! But I don't get to create the mountains; that's been left to a higher authority than I. So, I have to go in search of them. It's much the same with the Rules of

Fundraising. Neither you nor I get to make them. They just exist, and we must persevere until we find them.

Speaking of perseverance, as a novice fly fisherman, weeds can be a daunting enemy. I have to confess, frustration and fulmination abound when I'm fishing among them. They reach out and grab my backcast more times than not. The small river becomes just a narrow corridor with weedy little hands reaching out to grab every movement of my fly line. Tangles and anxiety usurp the peace and serenity associated with the sport. Sometimes my fishing line just ends up in a bad, tangled mess.

That's when I take a deep breath and recite the mantra of all fly fishermen: "Tangles are just part of the process." The trick now is to calm myself down. The fish will still be there waiting; I just need to concentrate on the tedium of releasing my fly from the spaghetti-like mass of fishing line.

This is when I begin to think seriously about cutting the line and just re-rigging and starting over. But I also remind myself that this is a part of the sport and learning how to get out of a mess that I alone have created is a discipline that I need to master.

This is fundraising too! As you know, it involves a great deal of preparation, entanglements, an extreme amount of patience and discipline. If I could make a weedless world, I'd do it, at least during fishing season, but like with the Rules of Fundraising, I don't have a vote. However, the joy of accomplishing our mission is worth all the tangles and the weeds.

It requires a passion for your cause and for the sense of fulfillment that comes from carefully using the budget dollars entrusted to your care to become a master craftsman of philanthropy. Knowing your limitations, where instinct and intelligence can lead you astray, is a place many well-meaning people are afraid to go. It says a lot about us, I guess. Sometimes we think we know something we really don't. Or perhaps we feel guilty because we've been hired to do something and we think we should know our craft better than we actually do. Worst case, it may feed our ego to be able to think we have the position and power to make up our own rules. As a fundraising consultant I see this kind of self- delusion much more often than I would like. For me it's one of the most heartbreaking experiences I encounter in my work.

When a board member, CEO or Director of Development begins to espouse their personal philosophy, I know we're all in trouble. It usually begins with a statement like this: "You see, our organization is unique..." I fell prey to it myself when I first started out, and it didn't serve me well. It's pretty embarrassing to end a year of working long and difficult hours and end up with a pouch full of glittering fool's gold.

So how do you ensure that you are discovering the time- tested Rules of Fundraising and not just somebody's personal opinion? Let's continue on down the road a bit and see where all of this leads...

RULE #4

"What you think you know about fundraising doesn't matter."

As sad as it is, it doesn't really matter what you or I want to think we know about a fundraising approach or strategy. It hurts just to write it. In fact, much of reality hurts; getting splinters, stubbing toes, getting a root canal, growing fat, growing old and fat...you get the idea. I'd like to think my life experience or my bachelor's and master's degrees count for something. Alas, with all sadness, they don't. What counts in fundraising and football is the score. Did my attempt to score put points on the board, or did I get sacked?

Experienced fundraisers know the awful truth of this rule. To continue with the sports metaphor, a coach who doesn't win doesn't keep his job. It's as simple as that. Your organization may like you, and I sincerely hope they do, but your board and CEO are evaluating you on your ability to provide financial resources for your cause, not on your undeniable passion for your mission (which is important) or the fact that you always bring donuts on Tuesdays (which for some of your less goal-oriented colleagues may be even more important).

Unfortunately "what we think we know about fundraising" is a cow patty many fundraisers can't resist stepping in! I can usually spot a person who's about to mess up their shoes within about 30 minutes of meeting them. One trait they all share is their need to make assumptions rather than ask questions.

Assumptions can get you smeared green from the top of your head all the way down to the bottoms of your feet, or at the very least, put slimy stuff between your toes, whereas questions can lead you to the places where the open pastures are.

Questions can help you determine the length and width of the field. They can help you determine the kind of cow patties ahead of you, empower you with knowledge that can determine if they're hard and white or soft and gooey, or at least lead you to a friendly farmer who can suggest an alternate path (like wading in the river). A good fundraiser knows that what they want to believe doesn't matter.

Ecclesiastes says it well, *"Vanity of vanities, all is vanity"* (Ecclesiastes 1:2, NKJV). If we want to follow the rules, it requires that we part with as much of our vanity as possible. I know my ego smarts at having to acknowledge that I even have an ego. But I do! And I suppose, like most of us, you do too. In order to follow the rules of effective fundraising we would be better served to unfasten all the buttons and belts of our ego, slide out of any psychological defenses we may have, and lay them gently on the ground. Fully exposed, we have to face the fact that we are defenseless. This is where the strength and wisdom are found, in our defenselessness.

In short, the best place to begin to learn the craft of fundraising is to admit to ourselves that we know very little and we are in need of much assistance. The good news is there are more resources available today than at any point in history. There are some great resources online, webinars, seminars, academies, clinics and even old-fashioned things likes books (which can quite easily be downloaded onto your Kindle or iPad). As for me, I'm of the generation that likes to buy books. That way I can write in them, dog-ear the important pages and interact with the author by writing notes in the margins. A few good books to know about are:

DIRECT MAIL:

Revolution in the Mailbox, Your Guide to Successful Direct Mail Fundraising
By Mal Warwick

MAJOR GIFTS:

Mega Gifts, Who Gives Them, Who Gets Them
By Jerold Panas (or anything else written by Jerry Panas)

The Artful Journey, Cultivating and Soliciting the Major Gift
By William T. Sturtevant

The Continuing Journey: Stewardship and Useful Case Studies in Philanthropy
By William T. Sturtevant

The Millionaire Next Door: The Surprising Secrets of America's Wealthy
By Thomas J. Stanley and William D. Danko

RELIGIOUS:

A Spirituality of Fundraising
By Henri J.M. Nouwen

FOUNDATION GRANT WRITING:

The Foundation Center's Guide to Proposal Writing
By Jane C. Geever

ADVANCED READING:

Positioning: The Battle for Your Mind
By Al Ries and Jack Trout

Innovate Like Edison: The Success of America's Greatest Inventor
By Michael J. Gelb and Sarah Miller Caldicott

SOME ASSOCIATIONS THAT OFFER A VARIETY OF EDUCATIONAL OPPORTUNITIES INCLUDE:

The Direct Marketing Association's Nonprofit Federation
www.nonprofitfederation.org

The Association of Fundraising Professionals
www.afpnet.org

The Christian Leadership Alliances' Development Track
www.christianleadershipalliance.org/page/ITI

National Catholic Development Conference
www.ncdc.org

Alliance of Lutheran Development Executives (ALDE)
www.alde.org

No one book, association or online opportunity will suffice. In fact I have found some pretty lousy information disseminated from presenters at the associations I belong to, but associations are improving in their selection of presenters, and most always, post-presentation surveys are conducted to help improve the quality of each year' s offerings.

I find I learn most from those who present specific principles, tactics and strategies and back them up with respectable research, results and/or case studies that reinforce their main points. Less helpful are those who present concepts that are unsupported by evidence or withheld until their services are purchased.

As the rule states, "What you think you know about fundraising doesn't matter." What we want to be true doesn't count. The only thing that matters is: Are our efforts effective?

RULE #5

"The rules apply to all nonprofits, even if you think your organization is 'unique.'"

This is a dicey little rule. I think I may have run into more trouble with this one than, perhaps, just about any other.

When I hear a trustee, president or development officer tell me that their organization is "unique," I shudder. I generally know what's coming next…her or his rules about not following the rules!

Now, I'm not so far gone that I'm totally unaware of the nuances and voices unique to each charitable cause. Every organization is unique. I fully understand this. What gets me into trouble is I must have some kind of messianic complex that keeps me from walking away from organizations who believe that they get to make their own rules.

One of the most common breaches of this rule of fund-raising is trying to be too subtle in asking your donors for money in a direct mail letter, e-mail blast, social media, or on-air spot (if you're using broadcast). This usually happens at the board level or when the copy or script is circulated to the CEO, who feels the pressure to back off from a very specific request for funding. (This is covered thoroughly in Rule #8.) The end result is a letter/post/online ad/e-mail/radio spot that does not communicate well or accomplish the expected income goals.

Now, why would anyone want to back off from a very specific "ask" or request for funding? We all know that no one intends to raise less money by making a less direct appeal, but this is the effect of the hesitancy to make a straightforward ask. It often happens when the person signing the letter (usually the CEO) has read the copy, sits back in her chair and asks herself, "What will my donors think if I send them communication that is this direct in its approach? We've not done this historically, so it will sound too brazen. I might get some complaints from board members or major donors."

Yes, she may be right. Perhaps a donor or a board member will call her and express their dissatisfaction with the tone of the communication. But the reality of the situation is, a more direct ask is much more likely to raise money than what we fundraisers call a "soft ask." This is when the CEO invokes the mother of all trump cards: "Our organization is unique. Our donors have never been communicated with in this fashion before, and I'm not going to start now." How can anyone on her staff stand up to this pronouncement? It tends to shut off all debate, and the uniqueness of the organization continues; never mind that the reason for using a more direct ask is directly related to the CEO's desire that more money be raised. A declaration of uniqueness is most often a cover for not being willing to do what must be done to increase income. It can be one of the most frustrating aspects of direct response fundraising. More money is being called for, but the methodology cannot change.

Putting it bluntly, to challenge this kind of thinking is akin to spitting into the wind. But there is hope. The uniqueness declaration can be challenged in an effective manner if two very critical components are in place:

1. The director of development, the board and the CEO have developed trusting relationships.
2. The director of development has the ability to communicate the severity of the board's or CEO's decision without being disrespectful.

One of the best lines I've ever heard in a situation like this was coined by my dear friend and colleague Wiley Stinnett.

I've heard him revert to this approach many times during our years of working together. He simply asks, "How much money do you want to lose?" Even Wiley doesn't win this one all of the time, but his track record is exceptional if he has built the trusting relationship needed for this kind of give and take.

It's important to know that an organization's uniqueness doesn't mean we get to create our own reality or rules. We can create our own culture, language and voice, but the rules are still there, and they must be followed to have the hope of success.

Board members can be a gift to their ministry by grappling with this rule and supporting the new directions required to meet their increased financial expectations. I have seen trustees who have killed the spirit of the development officers and those who have set the organization free to accomplish all that they have been called to accomplish. As a trustee, I challenge you to consider which kind of impact you'd like to make on the nonprofit that has been entrusted to you.

CEOs can be the advocate for change, in this regard, by seeking to know and understand The Rules of Fundraising themselves and providing training to their board to help them gain a positive perspective toward asking for gifts in a direct and truthful manner. The issue isn't "should we ask for funds"; rather it is "will we allow for the direct and measurable communication of opportunities to engage our donors?"

Truthfulness and accuracy should be the concern of leadership rather than the specifics of how funds are raised. This is why you have a development staff. You will serve best by governing least, especially in areas of great complexity like fundraising. If the organization you serve is unique only because you will not ask for gifts, you may find yourself in the same predicament as the biblical servant who, in the Parable of the Talents, decided to bury the talent that was entrusted to him in the ground for fear of the Master's rebuke (see Matthew 25).

RULE #6

"Effective fundraising is counter-intuitive."

In my mind, it's difficult to be an effective fundraiser. It requires a lot of insight and practice to become a true craftsman. If you've been in the field awhile you know this all too well. According to the rules, you've already been asked to give up your experience, your instinct, your ego, and now you're about to be asked to question your intuition. By this time you might be asking yourself, "What've I got left?" Oh, but you're honing your skills, sharpening your wits and learning the fine points of your trade. Most important of all, you are also humbling yourself before your God. Intuition can be kind of tricky. It can, when left to its own devices, disallow the necessary checks and balances of objective reality. One time I was fishing in a blizzard up in Wisconsin (speaking of denying reality). The snow was falling at a rate of about three inches per hour. But as most experienced fisherman know, lousy weather can produce some of the best results. So here I am in my chest waders,

approaching the bank of the Sheboygan River. Looking down at the edge of the water, I can see the white sandy bottom right next to the riverbank. I step carefully out onto the sand, and in a flash I'm floating up to my armpits in very cold, fast-moving water! What I thought was sand, in reality, was submerged ice! I'd broken through, and my feet were floating out into the current. As I fell, I quickly grabbed the branch of an unnervingly small tree and held on for dear life. Thankfully I had a safety strap fastened tightly around my chest. This is the only thing that prevented the icy water from filling my waders and taking me to the bottom of the river. It took some careful maneuvering for me to pull myself back to the shore.

Fortunately the frail-looking tree branch held as I placed my right foot up onto the frozen bank and pulled myself up to solid ground.

Everything in me said that I was stepping onto sand. That's what I mean by intuition being kind of tricky. It can prompt us to do things that we should never do.

Trusting our intuition can be like mistaking ice for sand. It is often the motivating force that leads a fundraiser to do things she believes but shouldn't be done, like suppressing her major donors from the normal streams of communication being offered to smaller donors. On the surface, this makes sense. Major donors are special people, and it's not a good thing to deluge them with direct mail, newsletters, e-blasts and all the other tools available in your fundraising toolbox.

Here's the counter-intuitive part. Many organizations are understaffed and therefore don't have the ability to provide personal contact or communication to every one of their major donors. **By suppressing normal streams of communication, they've unintentionally isolated the very people who need to know what their generous support is accomplishing!**

Intuition can lead us into making other costly mistakes too. Many development officers believe that it only makes sense to suppress major donors who've just given, from their next general giving opportunity. This leads me to another example of how trusting our intuition can keep us from being effective fundraisers.

Experienced fundraisers know, "The donor most likely to give is the one who has just given!" Yup! That's the rule.

Now, again, I don't get to have input into the formation of the rules; I just have to discover what the rules are and live by them. If you struggle with this rule, just know you are in great company!

Let's say today you receive a generous gift of $25,000 from Harry Smith. Now, it's a very nice gift. In fact it's one of his larger gifts to your organization. But, you were planning to approach Mr. Smith within the month with a request of $100,000 for the quiet phase of your new capital campaign. Your intuition light starts blinking in your left eye. It's telling you to hold off for a few months until a reasonable amount of time has passed.

But let's consider this oft-quoted fundraiser's story that circulates in the halls of evangelical philanthropy. D.L. Moody, the great Chicago evangelist, was very well-known among the prominent businessmen of the city. One day he walks into a large establishment and the owner sees him, rises from his office chair and comes out to greet him. They shake hands, and Moody is escorted back into the owner's office, where D.L. sits on the edge of his chair, leans forward and asks the owner for a gift. "Every time you come in here, Dwight, you ask me for a gift!" the owner quips. "Yes," Moody is said to have responded, "And every time you give!"

Sometimes it just bewilders me, but the fact is donors love to give. It makes them feel great inside. They also love to feel needed and included in the advancement of your cause.

Any well-trained capital campaign consultant will tell you that a respected peer of Mr. Smith's should approach him, thank him profusely for his generous support and then ask him for $250,000 for their campaign! That's right, 10 times the amount of his largest annual fund gift. Although it may be counter- intuitive, the best donor is one who has just given a gift.

This rule, of not leaning too heavily on our intuition, goes against our instincts. After all, we've all made good decisions by "trusting our gut." But in fundraising this can put you into a place you'd rather not be if it means that you ignore The Rules. That's what it means when the rule states: Effective fundraising is counter-intuitive.

A very practical example of the lack of knowledge of or the decision to ignore this rule is seen when a nonprofit is asking for money in any one of the many channels available to us today. It is all too common to see a fundraising letter make the case for a vital need only to end the letter without specifically asking for a gift! (I think I lost most of my hair over this one!)

Intuition leads us to hesitate to "close the deal." Non-profits often feel a direct request for a specific amount of money is simply just too strident. I implore you; please trust the wisdom of the ages when it comes to this. Donors will generally do what you ask them to do. If you ask them to pray about this need, that's just what they'll do. But if you ask them to thoughtfully consider giving a gift of $150 today, they are most likely to respond just as you've asked. Fundraising is indeed counter-intuitive, and it is the wise trustee, CEO or development officer who will let go of their fear of offending donors and be open and honest about why you are writing to them; you need their financial support.

RULE #7

"The only thing that matters is does it work."

When I began my company, I had just moved into a nice little house in Wheaton, Illinois.

I had new living room furniture that had been ordered from a catalog. It was inexpensive, and what I thought we needed at the time. The day the furniture truck pulled up on our tree-covered street it was very exciting...for about 10 minutes. After the two hefty delivery guys placed it in our living room and left, the whole family immediately sat down to enjoy the forest green leather couch, love seat and armchair. We all slid off! I mean it, literally. The stuffing in the furniture was bulging and massive to the point that we couldn't stay on the slippery stuff! We sat there on the floor looking at each other, and my wife laughing said, "This isn't going to work, is it? I'm never going to order furniture from a catalog ever again." It was fun listening to her on the telephone talking with the furniture company: "I'm sorry, you'll have to come take it away; it's not possible to sit on it. We keep falling off!" It simply didn't work.

Building a quality development program can take several years to complete. I've found that it doesn't come overnight and there are few shortcuts, if any. Mostly it's learning the tricks of the trade, using the right tools and serving in the apprenticeship of time. It also requires having the ability to see the potential of something that perhaps others can't see.

I remember, while working for a relief and development organization, that we had our backs to the wall. We were terribly short on money, and we had run out of year. I decided to send a U.S. Post Office Priority Mail package with a hard- hitting letter requesting year-end gifts. The package and postage cost was $2.50 each. I knew it was a bit of a public relations gamble, but the situation demanded it. Sure enough, we raised $250,000 at a cost of $15,000. It was a joyous success...but I got a phone call from an irate donor, who had responded to the mailing with a gift of $2,000. She called to inform me that this was a terrible waste of money and she didn't approve. I thanked her for her input, explained that this mailing was only sent to a select group of faithful friends (which it was) and promised to never send her another package of this type ever again. I hung up the phone, shook my head and reveled in the fact that this woman gave $2,000 at a cost of $2.50 and that she would not have responded unless I had done something extraordinary to gain her attention and her gift. I immediately flagged her name indicating to NOT send this type of package to her ever again and celebrated our success with the rest of our staff. The truth is, it was a great use of donated dollars, and I would do this again when the situation called for it…because it worked!

Just a word of caution here: this isn't an approach that will work if it is used too often. It's something to be saved for desperate times. We needed something that was going to raise significant amounts of cash in a short period of time. We did just that. It worked.

In considering what works, I remember all too clearly something from when I first became a fundraiser. While working in this new position, I learned several important lessons. One of the critical things I learned was that preparing to fundraise is necessary; there must be a vision and a plan. But I also learned that there comes a time to stop preparing and start implementing!

Sitting in my little closet-sized office, I began noticing that I could move paper all day long and it wouldn't raise a penny. There were forms for everything; forms to fill out for vacations, expense report forms, purchase order forms and even forms to request more forms! After filling out papers all day, usually in triplicate, my angst began to overwhelm me. How could I spend all day shuffling paper and have any sense of accomplishment? The hungry and hurting people of the world needed my help, and this wasn't doing anything for them.

I began to learn that I was falling into an insidious trap that can happen to any fundraiser. It was right up there with just talking a good game.

My volume of activity looked good, but it wasn't helping donors take out their checkbooks or their credit cards and actually give! There were no transactions taking place when I was sitting in endless committee meetings, having birthday parties for staff or any of the other cultural aspects of working in a nonprofit. I know this probably made me look like the curmudgeon I fear I can be, but I began to realize that moving the ball was the only way to score. In fact, I think it started to sink in that fundraising was going to require a certain amount of obsession to be successful.

Actually, in thinking about it, being obsessed with raising money is one of the nicer things I've been accused of. For me, it's actually a badge of honor. Over the years I developed the ability to spot effective development people by the way they use their time. They understand the value of time just as they understand the value of a check with lots of zeros from a major donor. Good development people are the ones you hear saying things like, "I wish I had a skateboard so I could get around this place faster." Imagine the scene in a newsroom just before deadline. Papers are flying, keyboards are rattling, people are yelling, copy is being proofed and all the time the clock is inching its way toward deadline. This is what a good development department looks like to this old set of eyes.

No type B personalities here! If you are a type B, you don't necessarily have to worry. Just make certain that you have at least one type A around who is driving things on a day-to- day basis. **This is an area where the board and CEO can lend a hand. They can ensure that there is a high- energy person in the development department who has the personality and authority to act.**

Sometimes speed is critical, but only if we know where we're headed. I've seen a lot of development officers who did not understand the difference between moving paper, checking e-mail, text messaging, tweeting, using Facebook and raising money. I believe it's the difference between developing a craft and decorating an office.

If you'll permit me one other observation here, before we move on, I'd like to make a comment about a widely used time killer that most often doesn't work; i.e., special events. If we're not careful, we can allow special events to consume more time than they're worth. I've had to learn to choose carefully where to invest my limited time, in a silent auction that eats my lunch for weeks or months only to raise $3,000, or a special event like a golf outing that can raise hundreds of thousands of dollars.

Now, I'm NOT a golfer, but even I respect the fundraising value of a well-planned and executed golf outing. Awhile back I had a dear friend, the president emeritus of one of our oldest and most beloved homeless causes, call to thank me for my contribution to their annual golf outing. They had raised $934,000; now that's moving the ball! It worked! And that's what matters in fundraising!

RULE #8

"The 5 commandments of offer development must be followed."

The sages of our craft have taught me that people need compelling reasons to give. The rules are very specific about this. Now, if I could write the rules, I'd change this one. A lot more money could be raised for great causes if this rule didn't exist. In fact, many development officers don't even know about this rule. So if you know and live by this one you have a distinct advantage over those who don't know it or who choose to ignore the following 5 commandments of offer construction:

1. Thou shalt always state what problem or opportunity your organization is trying to solve. e.g., people are dying due to lack of food, shelter and medical care.

2. Thou shalt always tell your donors how your organization plans to solve the problem or take advantage of the opportunity. e.g., food is available, and distribution channels are in place.

3. Thou shalt always know and communicate how much money your organization needs to solve your problem or seize your opportunity. e.g., the total cost to provide the food.

4. Thou shalt always tell the donor how their gift will solve the problem or help you take full advantage of the opportunity. e.g., you can feed one person for $6.00 per day (using your own real numbers of course).

5. Thou shalt always tell the donor why it is important for them to give today to solve the problem or seize the opportunity. e.g., XX,XXX people in this area go to bed hungry every night.

My feeble attempt at sacredness here is only to make the rather strong point that a development officer ignores these commandments at his or her own peril. These commandments apply to every channel of fundraising communication used.

Websites, e-blasts, social media, radio, TV, brochures, newsletters, telemarketing, direct mail cultivation to existing donors, new donor acquisition and major donor proposals all require the application of these 5 commandments. Yes, you can raise small amounts of money without using them. Yes, you can use some of these commandments and still raise some money. But if all five of these commandments are applied, religiously, significant increases in income for your cause await you. This is so very important that I'm willing to risk sounding preachy on this rule.

Following this rule has totally revolutionized many organizations' development programs. I have seen ministries and charitable causes of all types benefit from this knowledge. It doesn't matter if they're committed to Preserving the Hedgehog, Eliminating Canker Sores or Saving the Inch Worm, these commandments will increase net income and impact society for good. There's a little job security involved here too!

A few years ago we were hired by a well-known international Christian ministry to assist them with their direct mail program. Our efforts started off strong and then began to taper off. After several attempts at change and close review of their letter copy, we realized that we had strayed away from this rule. Upon discovery, we quickly corrected our course, and the income picture improved significantly and has remained strong to this day.

I read this rule to our Senior Vice President for Strategic Insights, Wiley Stinnett, whom I quoted earlier. He has over 50 years experience in discovering and applying the rules. He listened attentively, commenting here and there, and then repeated something I've heard him say many times, **"People not only do not follow the 5 commandments, they've made up their own commandment: They have convinced themselves that people will give to their cause simply because their organization has a need."** There is great wisdom here. The fact is every nonprofit exists to meet needs; so need alone won't move a donor or prospective donor to action. The 5 Commandments, or what we refer to on a daily basis as The Principles of Effective Offer Construction, are absolutely necessary to maximize income for your cause. It clearly requires much thought and practice to master this skill of creating an effective offer, but you'll be so pleased with the results that once experienced you'll never want to turn back.

RULE #9

"You don't have to lie to raise money."

This may seem like an unnecessary rule in philanthropic work... I only wish it were! The vast majority of nonprofits are very worthy and upright in their fundraising practices. Unfortunately, there are some serious scams out there!

That's why many states are, at the time of writing, requiring the registration of nonprofits (41) and consultants to nonprofits (24). I only expect this number to increase in the coming years. We have a law firm that specializes in keeping us current in this process. Since I have to sign all of the registrations and pay the fees, I know we're in compliance. What's interesting, however, is the number of new clients we serve who are NOT current in their registrations. It's now a regular part of our new client onboarding process to ensure they are up-to-date in all of the state registrations that apply. If you're wondering how to ensure that you are properly registered in every state where you solicit funds, you can run a select of all the states where you have donors or intend to acquire them. After you've done this, simply contact the Secretary of State or Attorney General's office and they'll direct you to the proper forms to complete, or go to *www.multistatefiling.org.*

Annual fees currently range from $25-$800, depending upon the state. By the way, fines for disregarding the registration of your organization range from $1,000-$10,000, per violation per state!

Looking beyond all things legal, you and I both know that it's also important to protect your organization from all ethical breaches and scandal in general. Ultimately this task falls to your board of trustees, however, any hint of unethical or scandalous activity can create a fundraising maelstrom from which it may take years to recover. Those organizations who have "slipped" in the public's eye can tell you the bitter truth of this statement.

The heartbreaking part of many ethical breaches is that they are totally unintentional, just like letting your organization's state registrations lapse. There is often no outright desire to lie or mislead, but when a good "story" gets into the wrong hands...fasten your seatbelt; it's going to be one of the most frightening off-road experiences of your life! Let me give you an example: A social services organization in a well-known Western city asked the public to gather personal hygiene items for the poor. They were given boxes with the organization's campaign name and logo on them. Hundreds, if not thousands, of people responded by filling these boxes with socks, underwear, soap, deodorant and many of the other things less-fortunate people need and seldom receive.

The community was generous in both filling the boxes and delivering them to the designated drop-off points. The warehouse began to pile up with blue boxes of heartfelt generosity. The charity's plan was to distribute these boxes during the holiday season. Now, all of us are flawed in some way, as was the executive director of this organization. He was very busy and failed to issue the directive to begin distributing the boxes. It wasn't intentional, but the consequences were devastating.

Enter an ambitious local news reporter who was seeking to gain national media attention as an investigative reporter. A disgruntled ex-employee informed the reporter of the executive director's oversight. You see what's coming. The reporter picked up the scent and pursued the story like the bloodhound he was. The news report made it sound as if the organization was intentionally collecting gifts-in-kind from the community with no intention of honoring the donors' purpose of helping the less fortunate. Financial donations shut off like the light bill hadn't been paid. In the ensuing weeks and months the organization lost roughly 50% of its donor base! Sadly, other than the executive director, it was the poor of this great city who suffered the most.

It was not a lie that tripped up this well-intentioned leader. His inaction may well have been unintentional and was certainly mismanagement, but to the reporter it was just too good to pass up. To him the scoop became a plot to exploit the good intentions of the public.

One more media story, and then I'll move on. Another social services group in a major Southern city found itself "staked out" by a "yellow journalist." He drove his SUV into their parking lot, placed a used television on the organization's loading dock and began filming. He was hoping to catch an employee stealing a "donated" item so he could make the evening news.

Sure enough, an employee emerged from the building and picked up the TV and placed it in the trunk of his car. He went back inside the building only to re-emerge after a few minutes and drive off.

As soon as the employee's car left the lot, the journalist and his cameraman leapt from their vehicle and confronted the manager of this facility with their "evidence." "Oh, that was Henry," replied the manager, "He asked permission to deliver the TV to our recovery facility where a family has been hoping for a television to watch in the evening. I gave him my permission."

After examining the documentation of this transaction thoroughly, the reporter and his cameraman cursed and left.

My point here isn't to question the freedom of the press. Rather, it's to remind us all of the vulnerability of appearances. A lie needn't be deceptive speech or actions but merely the perception of a lie.

Lying isn't something any of us want to do, yet sometimes it happens. Have you noticed that the people who lie the most are the ones who take the greatest offense at having their integrity questioned? You can usually tell who they are because, "methinks they doth protest too much!"

Lying in fundraising can certainly be unintentional, or maybe, to put it in more generous terms, "unconscious." Here are a few of the lies we often hear from some organizations:

1. Overstate the impact of their organization.
2. Tell their donors that they can't do their work without them. (This belies the fact that God is our provider through them.)
3. Create an emergency in order to raise more money.
4. Promise something to their donors and then don't deliver it.
5. Distort the facts of an appeal or a proposal.
6. Raise designated money and spend it somewhere else without telling the donor.
7. Use photographs and/or stories that are not from their organization without telling the donor.
8. Approach donors with a matching gift follow-up request when the match has already been met.
9. Inflate the magnitude of their need or opportunity. (e.g., we're going to end hunger in our world.)
10. Try to trick the donor into opening an email or envelope with something that is misleading.

Donors are intelligent people; I've found they will understand our circumstances if we'll just take the time to explain our situation in simple, honest terms. I've made phone calls to major donors and explained that we have just completed funding the project they have just now given to. In every case, I asked them if they would like their gift returned or if we could re-designate it. None of them has ever asked for their gift to be returned! They loved having the option to direct their giving, but once they had released the funds into our care they were happy to have us use it where it was most needed.

Most donors are just looking for the simple truth. My own philosophy of the ethics of fundraising is quite simple. If I find myself trying to justify something or, perhaps another way to say it is, if I find myself looking for a way to "spin" something, then I'm treading on thin ice. I have never regretted doing the right thing; i.e., going the extra mile to ensure there is no sense of shadiness in raising funds. It's not only the right thing to do, but there just might be an unethical reporter looking for a good story.

RULE #10

"Any good idea is worth stealing."

I've done it, and perhaps you have too! I've seen an e-mail, social post, direct mail package or even an ad campaign that I know has been extremely successful, and I've pilfered the idea. That's how I've built my toolbox of great tactics over the years. Now I know it seems a bit strange to have this rule follow one about ethics and not telling lies to raise money, but I think you'll see the difference right away…and besides, what decent book about fundraising doesn't have at least one appearance of a flip-flop?

Who invented the Emergency Gram? I certainly don't know, but I'd like to find them and plant a big sloppy kiss on 'em! Over the years I've raised millions of dollars for worthy causes, with legitimate emergencies, through this "borrowed" approach.

Again with Ecclesiastes:

"That which has been is what will be That which is done is what will be done And there is nothing new under the sun. Is there anything of which it may be said, "See this is new?" It has already been in ancient times before us."
Ecclesiastes 1:9-10, NKJV

Now, "ancient times" may be 2001 for you; it really doesn't matter. I began my life of thievery in the 1980s and haven't been able to overcome it yet. I actually think I'm addicted to it! I'm constantly on the lookout for my next shoplifting opportunity.

I've stolen donor acquisition ideas, website ideas, telemarketing ideas, and perhaps my personal favorite, competitor's ideas. Not through industrial espionage, mind you, but through watching to see what ideas are used year after year. I figure, if an organization is using the same approach over and over again there are only two options:

1. They're stupid (which is highly unlikely).
2. They know what they're doing.

Once I discover a good idea (one that appears to be following the rules), I like to take it, rework it just enough to make it my own, and then test it against the best ideas I've ever stolen! It's really an exhilarating process; you should try it. After all there's no direct response prison, purgatory or hell for thieves of this sort.

It was Mark Twain who said, *"It all began with Adam. He was the first man to tell a joke—or a lie. How lucky Adam was. He knew when he said a good thing, nobody had said it before. Adam was not alone in the Garden of Eden, however, and does not deserve all the credit; much is due to Eve, the first woman, and Satan, the first consultant."* - Notebook, 1867

On a more serious note, there are so many great ideas for fundraising available in the marketplace, it is to your advantage to begin collecting ideas as you encounter them and put them in a file for verification of their success. Because you are working in a nonprofit, a phone call to the organization that used this approach may well yield a friendly colleague who is more than happy to share their results with you. If the results are solid, and you have the numbers to prove it, I recommend moving this from the idea file into your proven concepts file. Not only can this help you to strengthen your lineup of good fundraising ideas, but the numbers can be a very helpful selling point to your CEO. Most of the truly great fundraising ideas in the marketplace have been borrowed and shared so many times that they have become staples in most fundraisers' repertoire. Remember, you are not in this alone; there is a very generous community of development officers who love nothing more than helping others (especially if your nonprofit is not perceived as competition). Which brings me to my last point: You are going to want to develop a culture of sharing on your part too. This creates an attitude and culture of openness in your organization and serves others who share your values.

RULE #11

"A good idea is a dime a dozen... but execution is everything."

Several years ago I had the privilege of having lunch with two very experienced fundraisers that I admire very much, Michael Johnson and David Genn. They've known each other for years, having worked together on the staff of The Slavic Gospel Association. It's a great work among the people and churches of the former Soviet Union. They got together at every opportunity, and I was honored to be invited to join them for lunch.

We were all three talking away in Pal Joey's Italian Restaurant when somebody said, "Good idea!" Now this is the language of fundraising.

You'll hear phrases like this whenever two or more are gathered together. Upon hearing the phrase, the two men spontaneously broke into the chant, "A good idea is a dime a dozen, execution is everything!" They spoke it like a song, a mantra even. David lifted his arm in the air, made a fist and brought his elbow down and the song home with the word "execution." Then they laughed together as only two journeymen can; eyes fixed and shared experiences transmitting back and forth through the soul-warming camaraderie bred only through the test of time. It was clear to me that they had shared the heart thrills and heartbreaks on the road to advance their life's work...raising money for something they love.

Now, I can't think of much a person can buy today for "a dime a dozen," paper clips maybe? All they can do is hold paper together unless you need to unwind one to use in the resetting of your PalmPilot™, or are those things obsolete now? I forget.

What isn't obsolete is this "ancient" rule. In my bespeckled eyes, "execution" is the process that enables a concept or idea to become action. I know at one point in the life of our firm, we identified 139 specific steps to create an appeal letter. The ability to execute is often what separates the short-term development officer from one with a future. I've seen not-for-profit leadership patiently tolerate someone who executes, even if they fail during many of their attempts. There's a great book called *Innovate Like Edison* that can tell you more about this than I can, but it was Thomas Edison who said, "I have not failed. I've just found 10,000 ways that won't work," before he founded what eventually became General Electric. In Edison's approach, failure didn't exist, because all outcomes yielded further data that he believed would ultimately provide a solution. Max DePree, former Chairman of the Board of the innovative furniture company Herman Miller, in his insightful book, *Leadership Jazz*, uses a phrase that I have come to cherish, "The yeast of failure."

How do we reconcile failure with the awful truth of Rule #7, "The only thing that matters is does it work?" If you are new to fundraising or have just accepted a position at a nonprofit, you may only have 18 months to prove yourself. You might ask, "Why 18 months?" Some of the master craftsmen of fundraising might well have their own thoughts here, but mine is: This is the length of time it takes for an organization to discover that the director of development talks a good game but can't raise money. It's also the time that it takes for an effective director of development to figure out that her organization wants her to raise money, but they want her to do it without following the rules. But just wait, there's more good news coming. In my experience, this means the clock is not on your side. Some fundraisers become paralyzed by this pressure, yet others are motivated by it. I've seen this to be the great proving ground of a person's character. It's simply not enough to have great ideas.

You have to prioritize your ideas, giving most of your energy to those strategies and tactics that you know will work. Remember, all you have to do is "execute" or move the ball enough to get a 1st down. This will buy you more time. Progress and hope are what board members and CEOs are looking for and need in a competent development officer. If you find yourself in one of these roles, the following may benefit you as you develop expectations for a new development officer.

If I were to put together a performance timeline for myself, I think it would look something like this: Set appropriate expectations **before I accept the position**. This is the time when I have the greatest leverage. (Hopefully this guidebook can give you some assistance with this.) Present my expectations and strategic plan to the CEO before I accept the position. This will buy me more time.

Once I accept the job, the approach that I've seen to be effective for the first month is as follows:

DAY 0-START DATE:

I would gather ALL the data and information that I could. What aspects of my new employer's development program have been working well? What has not? I would begin my planning process to execute what has been working; I'd leave the other stuff for later.

START DATE-DAY 5:

I'm going to want to allocate my time carefully. I don't think I'd give myself the luxury of a lot of "getting-to-know-the-organization" meetings or lunches. I know some are unavoidable, but I have to get something in the works right away. I think I'd use what I've learned before I officially started to formulate my plan for the first 30 days.

DAYS 6-12:

No free Saturdays for me for at least 60 days! I'd use this critical time to formulate my 30-day plan for approval. While I'm building my plan, I'd make certain my gift acknowledgement systems are working properly. All thank-you letters should be **snail-mailed** within 24-48 hours of receiving a donor's gift. I'd make certain these letters thank the donor for their contribution, ask for another gift and include a reply envelope. I would mail them ALL 1st class! Yes, this costs more, I know, but first-class postage guarantees in-home arrival dates of 1-5 days and provides me with any address changes that have been submitted to the U.S. Post Office. If my new employer has been taking 1-2 weeks to do data entry and sending out thank-you letters, I'll not only be creating immediate cash flow but improving relationships with donors as well (the big boss will like it too)!

DAYS 13-19:

I would present my plan to my supervisor on Day 13. All of my enthusiasm, focus and effort will go a long way toward showing my leadership progress and hope. Using Days 13-19 I would develop specific individual tactics for each of the strategies in my approved plan. This is where I have to caution myself against the temptation to be all speed and no direction. In my thinking, it would be important to execute or launch any portion of the plan that I can while I'm still completing the remaining tactics! For example, if I know I have an income-producing newsletter due in a month, I would get it started now. I would use this same strategy concurrently with the remainder of my planning. This applies to direct mail appeals too! The object here is for me to get money in the door as effectively and quickly as possible. In my hurry-up offense I don't want to forget the 5 Commandments in all that I do (Rule #8). Hope and progress, as well as several thousand dollars, will get me to a first-down position.

DAYS 20-26:

I'd use this valuable time to complete my tactics, making certain that ALL income sources are accounted for (see Rules #15 and 16). Now, before the majority of the money starts to come in, I'd use this time to ensure my data entry is being done correctly (including the coding) and begin compiling reports for the income that has begun to flow. So I don't meet myself coming and going, I think I'd break off a few hours to create an "integration chart" for all communication and fundraising sources so I can see any areas where donors are being overwhelmed or neglected. Using my chart, I'd make adjustments accordingly.

A note to self here: The temptation to get sidetracked by unfruitful special events can be overwhelming. The pressure will be mounting from volunteers, auxiliaries or advisory boards by this time. Everybody will have mountains of ideas for me, and they'll send me up a dead-end trail if I let them.

DAYS 27-33:

Only now would I begin thinking about major donors. This is where my most cost-effective gifts will come from. I know that many development officers make the mistake of isolating major donors from normal communication streams (like direct mail) while intending to develop a plan and strengthen relationships with their major donors. From my experience, I know the pressures of the job often prevent this from happening in a timely manner. The resulting isolation of major donors does me more harm than good, so I have included them in all my efforts to date.

I think I would select all major donors who have given $250 or more within the last 12 months ($100+ if my organization is on the small side) and then I would send them a special major donor proposal. I know the elements of this proposal must include the 5 Commandments of Rule #8!

1. A one-page, personalized cover letter
2. A one-page, personalized proposal (including a specific gift amount based upon their largest gift in the past 12 months)
3. A one-page reply device with several options for giving (e.g., a gift now, a quarterly or annual pledge)

4. A 9" X 12" carrier envelope, with handwritten name and address and 1st class postage (yes, I know it's expensive)

5. A #9 reply envelope (this can have a postage stamp applied for them)

Now the most important part of this strategy, my staff and I will call them within 7-10 days and do the following:

1. Ask if they received our proposal.

2. Ask if they have any questions about the proposal.

3. Ask if they think they'll be able to help. (I won't make a specific "ask" here; I'll let the proposal do the talking!)

Then, just for a moment, I'll sit back, enjoy the moment and count the money; hopefully I've just scored a touchdown! With a sigh, I'll slowly get up and get ready for the next game... no unemployment line for me!

RULE #12

"If you want something done right, DON'T do it by yourself."

Fundraising is truly a community building exercise. People ask, people give and people receive; everyone benefits. This rule requires that we remember the value of community.

Everything we do as fundraisers is to save or change the lives of people, be it in our neighborhood, church, town, city, state or province, country or the world at large. It's an exciting and fulfilling adventure, so much so that many are leaving their corporate careers to engage in causes that both delight and challenge them.

I remember a flight many years ago where I was seated next to a woman who worked for a commercial advertising agency. This was before personal earphones, smart phones,

Wi-Fi on airplanes and the iPad, so people still talked to each other. It seems, since we were both involved in enterprises that influenced people to take action, we had much in common. I also remember the statement this advertising executive made after I had described some of the wonderful things the clients I served were accomplishing in the world. She quietly said, "It's a heckuva lot better than what I do, trying to get people to buy beans and franks." And then she looked down at her hands, laying there in her lap, and sighed. We indeed have exhilarating lives accomplishing extraordinary feats for people whom God cherishes. We also have the ability and option of working in community.

The "fundraising community" is a community within the larger not-for-profit community. If you believe what you've read so far, you know there are special rules governing this unique and highly skilled community.

This rule is important in that it is intended to empower you to collaborate with those within your organization, as well as your peers in the fundraising community. It also assists you in the utilization of your fundraising consultant, if you have one.

We've all grown up hearing the expression, "If you want something done right, do it yourself." Granted, there are times when this applies, but I find it seldom works in fundraising, because fundraising is *counter-intuitive*. The great field of philanthropic encouragement is best done in community. If you're a development officer, this is an excellent opportunity to involve the board and/or your CEO. You'll need to know their approved vision and goals for the year in order to craft an appropriate strategic plan and budget. I wouldn't draw them into the weeds here, but knowing the big picture is essential.

This is especially true when it comes to the process of budgeting for income and expenses for our fundraising endeavors. You see, we need each other to challenge our observations, assumptions and calculations in the formation of something as critical as a fundraising expense budget or an anticipated income forecast. I prefer the term "forecast" rather than income budget here because it resembles a weather report more than an accounting process. The weather can change radically overnight ,and so can the forces impacting fundraising. While this may not feel particularly comforting, it is true just the same.

It's also important that we manage the expectations that our organization has about our ability to generate income. Managing expectations and "perceived promises" are things that investment firms have been careful to develop over the years.

Granted, this may largely be due to the regulations of the Securities Exchange Commission (SEC), but it is now a standard practice among investment firms.

So, how do we apply their qualified expectations to our organization? First, I found it helpful to ask myself if my current methods and presentations of expense and income forecasting may, unintentionally, be working against the long-term credibility of my department.

Here are a few guidelines I've learned and used over the years to ensure that I'm living in reality:

1. Plan plenty of time for my income and expense forecasting (use the due date for my budget and work backwards, laying out a timeline for deliverables within my department)

2. Obtain income goals from my leadership team (without committing anything at this point)

3. Determine all of my current income sources (here is a general list many not-for-profits use):
    - White mail (anything that cannot be attributed to a specific initiative)
    - Planned giving
    - Receipt income (from thank-you letter bounce backs)
    - Major gifts

- Special events (organization and donor/volunteer initiated)
- Banquets
- Gifts in kind
- Product sales
- Fees
- Seminars
- Recruitment (students, campers, missionaries and volunteers)
- Thrift stores (soliciting donated goods and marketing)
- Car sales
- Corporate giving
- Grants
- Capital campaigns
- Online donations
- Mobile giving
- Radio/TV
- Electronic Funds Transfers (EFTs)
- Honorariums
- Direct mail
- Monthly giving clubs
- Scholarships
- Newsletters
- Annual reports
- Donor acquisition
- Annual campaigns

4. Document everything carefully. I don't want to have my memory conflict with my supervisor's memory; I'll lose

5. Draw deeply from the historic information at my disposal

6. Examine current conditions to inform my historic performance

7. Build my forecast brick by brick; don't take the easy way out by simply adding a percentage of increase over the previous year

8. Do the hard work of obtaining reliable data; again I don't want to give in to the human impulse of approximating or guessing

9. Establish detailed assumptions for each income source

10. Test my assumptions through "group think" (use my team here)

11. Determine the new strategies I want to test

12. Gather hard data from my fundraising community for test strategies

13. Once my strategies are determined, I will need to determine detailed creative, programming and print specifications for each one of them

14. Use my detailed specifications to obtain pricing from my vendors, agencies or consultants

15. Compile all of the information I've gathered up to this point

16. Let the reality of my hard work determine my income forecasts and expense budgets.

17. Now, I find it best to step back and compare my work to that of previous years. I call this my reality check

18. Be careful of what I forecast (read promise)

19. Ask myself if I've been too optimistic or too conservative in my income projections. If I have, I need to go back into the detail and rebuild it (this is why I need plenty of time)

20. Establish my "level of confidence" in my plan (90%, 80%, whatever), then I'll reforecast accordingly

21. Invite trusted and knowledgeable colleagues, advisors and consultants to review my work

22. Make whatever revisions necessary

23. Compare my income and expense projections against leadership goals

24. Anticipate the questions that will arise during the presentation of my plan; prepare accordingly

25. Schedule my presentation and arrive totally prepared to be challenged and stretched

There, that's all there is to it! I hope you can see why you don't want to try to do all of this by yourself. There are far too many pieces to this planning process in which a person can miss something or overlook the fact that assumptions were made that could derail the whole thing. We need others around us who can contribute and challenge us to excellence, including our CEO and board.

RULE #13

"Get help when you need it."

Why are so many organizations looking for outside help? I've seen two main categories for organizations that are looking: those who are doing all of their own fundraising in-house and those who currently have an agency. In either case there are several reasons for wanting to make a change, but some of the most commonly expressed by CEOs and development officers are:

THOSE WHO ARE DOING EVERYTHING IN-HOUSE:

1. I need to focus more on the major gift portion of my portfolio. I don't have time to handle all of the other aspects of fundraising.
2. We are so short-staffed there is no way I can handle everything.

3. I'm too close to it; people won't listen to me because I'm on staff. I need someone to come in from the outside to tell them what to do. They'll listen to a consultant.

4. I'm doing three jobs already; there's no way I can do justice to any of them!

5. Our organization is in the business of helping people who are in trouble, not the technical side of the fundraising business. We certainly raise funds, and do a good job for the most part, but we're not experts at everything.

6. We simply don't know what we're doing! (This is usually a CEO, CFO or board member.)

7. We need to acquire new donors, and everything we've tried thus far hasn't worked very well.

8. There are so many new channels and opportunities available. I can't be an expert in all of them. I know we're leaving money on the table.

9. We're planning to launch the quiet phase of a $50 million capital campaign. It's going to be all-consuming for the next three years. I need help with keeping the rest of our development program on track.

10. We generally have a handle on the basics, but I need a trusted partner to come in, stand beside me and show

me how to avoid trouble and help us maximize our income.

THOSE WHO HAVE AN EXISTING RELATIONSHIP WITH A FUNDRAISING FIRM:

1. I like them, they're great people, especially our assigned representative, but our income has been flat for the last three years.
2. It feels like I have to pull them along when it comes to new ideas. I want them to be proactive and bring new strategies to us!
3. Analytics? What analytics? What I get is more like a monthly statement of where we are financially. And speaking of statements, their bill is always on time!
4. I think they've really changed. They're not the same company that I hired five years ago. It seems like it started when they were bought by that other company.
5. Their production time is way too long! It feels like I have to give them my data months before the mail date. By that time, a lot has changed; new donors have come onto our file and others have asked to be removed from our mailing list. Why does it take so long to produce a mailing?

6. They're a good company. The numbers are decent. I just think they've lost a step over the years. They've become somewhat complacent, maybe it's because they've lost so much talent to turnover.

7. I feel like I'm working for them and not the other way around! It seems like there is a little arrogance to them. I feel like they "talk down" to our staff.

8. I don't think they really get who we are. They haven't been able to "capture our voice."

9. It seems like they go out and hire the youngest and most inexperienced people in the market and put them on my account.

10. We just have to find a way to lower our fundraising costs.

Do you recognize yourself in any of these statements? If you do, you might want to circulate this list (or the entire rule) to your development and leadership team. Have them put check marks beside all points that apply. I hope this will help you to take a survey of how others in your organization are feeling about your need for help.

Securing the services of a suitable consulting firm can appear daunting at first, especially if you've never worked with one. The next rule might give you some guidelines to smooth this process.

RULE #14

"When it comes to consultants, you get what you pay for!"

Now this is the one rule we all know and have likely said ourselves at one time or another: you get what you pay for! But isn't it interesting that this phrase is generally used only after someone has gotten a good deal on something that turns out to be a dud!

Granted, we're all looking for bargains. That's just smart, and it makes our money go farther. I particularly envy the few people I know who get great deals on cars. I really don't know how they do it! I've only made one good deal that I can remember. I had a string of bad car deals going back, just before college, where I bought three $100 beaters in a row. My 29-year-old son, Graham, the car guy, tells me this is probably the equivalent to $1,000 cars in today's economy. Each one of them lasted for less than a month. All three were sold for junk.

But I revel in the memory of buying my first $500 car! It was a beauty, and it ran like a clock. It was a 1965 Plymouth Fury III. It had new tires and a rebuilt engine and was freshly painted in a slick metallic medium blue. Even the eight-track stereo system worked. (For any reader born after 1980, check with your parents; they'll explain this technology to you!) It ran well, and, aside from replacing a "u" joint in Santa Cruz, California, it never had any mechanical problems. I finally sold it for $300 during the 1974 gas crisis and bought a Toyota Corolla with a stick shift.

Since this book isn't "Car Buying for Dummies," I think you know where I'm headed. It stands to reason this same rule applies to increasing the quality of your development staff, investing in new technology, sending your staff to seminars to improve their performance or even hiring a fundraising firm.

Here are a few questions to guide you in improving the effectiveness and efficiency of your development department:

1. Have you identified the development areas where your organization performs well? What are they?

2. Have you identified the development areas where you perform more poorly than you would like? What are these?

3. What resources will it require to make the desired improvements in your department?

4. Can you quantify/justify the increased income that will result from making improvements? Be very specific.

5. If you're not sure what to do, seek professional counsel. If you decide to seek outside counsel (and many do) there are some important factors to consider.

I asked our former Senior Vice President/Chief Marketing Officer, Michael Johnson, who is now president of the Slavic Gospel Association, to share some of his insights into this process:

"My experience is that when a nonprofit conducts a review that includes more than one agency, they typically fall into the trap of making an agency selection based upon the wrong criteria.

"Specifically, they often choose a firm based upon an existing relationship with one of the nonprofit's leadership due to admiration of their work done for a similar kind of organization, cost issues, etc.

"However, if you make the wrong selection, it will only cost you in the long run in terms of lost revenue and the ongoing frustration that come with a bad and dysfunctional relationship. It is like a marriage; carefully pick the right partner and you'll enjoy years of joy and peace and prosperity.

"Therefore, prior to the search, sit down and make a list of those things that are most important to you and make sure that all the firms being considered are working from the same list. Be as objective as possible in your selection process.

"Remember, if you have an existing agency relationship (the one you want to sever) you probably chose them for the wrong reasons described above. Your ultimate selection needs to be based upon objective criteria that results in what is best for your organization.

"At our company, if someone asks for a proposal, we will conduct an extensive audit of their data file and then conduct on-site interviews with their senior management, the fundraising and marketing staff, and anyone involved in the strategic oversight, development and fundraising activities.

"If your potential consulting/partner does not do this, it will be difficult for them to identify both your strengths and challenges in order to develop an excellent proposal to serve your specific needs."

Here are a few questions to help you in finding a firm who will bring you a long, satisfying and profitable relationship:

1. Do you want to do a formal agency search using a Request for Proposal (RFP) process, or do you want to use a referral from a trusted peer? Do you have this option, or are you required by policy to use an RFP process?

2. Do you have an excellent RFP document? If not, you may want to ask respected peers for theirs. Most organizations are very willing to accommodate this request. An RFP document is simply a statement that outlines the scope of services that you are looking for in a consultant. One word of caution; resist the temptation to make this into a marketing tome. If it's too exhaustive in content and length you may not receive the comparative information you desire. Each consultant or consulting firm has their own language and definitions of those terms. Being concise in your RFP will enable you to more easily evaluate the answers you receive.

Once you have decided upon your approach (RFP or referral), you are going to want to make certain that you hire a firm that fits well with who you are, as well as what you need. Here are a few more questions to guide you in this process:

1. Do you like the people you are meeting with? Good chemistry with you and those you hire is critical in your search.
2. Are you looking for a vendor, an agency or a consulting/partner?

Vendor: If you have intentions of buying largely print production services and plan on developing the strategies, copy and creative in-house, this is probably your best bet. This is cheaper too. Just remember that you get what you pay for! Don't expect a vendor to know the Rules of Fundraising or teach them to you. They are most often a printing company or a mailing house. Be careful here though; most vendors know just enough about the Rules of Fundraising to be dangerous.

Agency: This type of firm is more of a classic advertising agency who specializes in direct response fundraising. Here you'll generally be assigned an account executive to liaise with your organization and the firm. It's strictly a business relationship. This kind of company will largely deliver the basic services at a reasonable price. You will need to lead them more than you would a Consulting/Partner (see below).

Consulting/Partner: This is a company that clearly seeks to know you, your cause and your donors. They demonstrate a passion for your cause *because they share your values.* A partner asks excellent questions and watches your back.

Fundraising, communications and marketing strategies are totally customized for your organization. A true partner can execute with great flexibility and responsiveness. This type of company places a high value upon meeting the overall needs of your organization; sometimes you may need help in areas other than development.

Partners will listen to you, lead you where you need it, stay out of the way when you've got it covered and serve you rather than dictate to you. Serving here means respectfully challenging you when you need it, not being an "order-taker." You maintain control while at the same time receiving solid counsel.

Most likely you'll find this kind of a relationship in a consulting/partner that thoroughly knows the Rules of

Fundraising and is willing to build into your organization by training you, your leadership and staff. Here, an experienced consultant rather than an account executive is assigned to you who is empowered to make recommendations and decisions on-site. A true partner brings other Subject Matter Experts (SMEs) to you so you are assured of the best possible thinking, execution and results. A true partner is generally more expensive than an agency, but...you do indeed get what you pay for, results that will significantly grow your organization!

RULE #15

"The greatest weakness of the nonprofit is only managing the expense side of the ledger."

As the story goes, this rule began in the form of a question that was put to a famous management guru. He was also a man of deep integrity and faith. Someone once had the foresight to ask him, "What is the greatest weakness of the nonprofit?" Rule #15 is my elaboration of his answer.

When I first heard this insight, I didn't fully understand what he meant, "They only manage the expense side of the ledger." I'm a bit challenged by balancing my checkbook.

But the longer I have served as a fundraising consultant for not-for-profit organizations and ministries, this concept has become much clearer.

As a consulting firm, it is both our privilege and respon-sibility to create value by offering insights, analytics, strate-gies and creative approaches to those we serve.

These services are most often offered in the form of rec-ommendations, which, as you know, may or may not be ac-cepted.

The rejection of a solid recommendation is one of the most difficult experiences a fundraiser or consultant has to face. It's devastating to watch as a proven strategy is left lying there on the table. There are usually two reasons for the rejection of a recommendation:

1. Expense
2. A low tolerance for risk (even calculated risk)

The more I experience these two factors the more I gain understanding of this rule.

Having served six years working in not-for-profit lead-ership, I am the first to admit there are many factors or pressures faced by organizations that are not always evi-dent to those of us on the "outside." One significant differ-ence between a not-for-profit and a for-profit entity is the not-for-profit is entrusted with allocating the expenditure of donated dollars. I see the prudence in maintaining this perspective. Often, when I encounter the question, "What would our donors say if they knew we were investing their gifts in this way?" This rule is a comfort to me here. It leads me to carefully and humbly ask, *"What would happen if a donor knew you had passed up a significant opportunity to invest in your organization's ability to deliver increased services, and you didn't take it?"*

The more I ponder it, I find myself asking, "So how does an organization decide between wise investments and high-risk ventures?" Now, I don't have a taste for Las Vegas, and I have no plans to go back. Gambling is not on my list of hobbies or addictions. In my thinking, an experienced fundraiser doesn't need to gamble. There are way too many other options available to philanthropy for this to be necessary, following the Rules of Fundraising not being the least of these.

I think you'll find that philanthropy is filled with generous people who are very willing to share ideas and best practices. I know that I personally find great joy in helping others who are seeking to grow in their craft. If I can help someone expand their repertoire with ideas, strategies and income—it makes me happy. As I have experienced it, philanthropy is about helping others and the beauty is—you don't lose anything by giving what you have to others.

People in our craft have been so very generous to me that it only seems like I'm continuing a loving tradition to do the same for people who are changing the world for good.

This is where CEOs and board members should perk up and take note. There is more to leading a nonprofit than accounting and thrift. One of the important concepts shared with me is, the significant difference between managing expenses and managing income in the growth of an organization. Managing expenses says, "How can we spend less and do the same or more?" while managing income says, "How should we best invest that which has been entrusted to us?" It seems to me that your nonprofit is really all about making an impact. If your organization needs and wants to make a maximum impact on your community, country and world it requires the wisdom to know when to conserve and when to invest.

Board members, CEOs and development officers that guide their causes into wise investments are every bit as valuable as a whole trainload of major donors. Has anyone ever told you this? If not, let me be the first to offer you this gift.

As I understand it, maximizing the impact of a cause requires intense focus on investments that enhance organizational effectiveness. Here are just a few questions to help you along your way:

1. Do I know what my goals are (both in the short and long term)?
2. Do I have specific, written strategies to accomplish these goals?
3. Do I believe the assumptions upon which my strategies are based?
4. How can I verify my assumptions if I have questions about them?
5. Do I need trusted counsel? Am I willing to seek it?
6. Are there ways I can test my assumptions without betting the farm?
7. If I have tested my assumptions, and believe them, do I have the authority, courage and faith to invest in moving forward?

It seems to me that the old management guru had making wise investments in mind when he made his now-famous declaration...

"The greatest weakness of the nonprofit is only managing the expense side of the ledger."

One quick story, then we'll move on. A media ministry we served needed to replace all of their outdated analog broadcasting equipment with digital gear. The cost for this extensive updating was substantial; $1.5 million. Our company proposed a campaign involving both direct mail and on-air fundraising at a cost of $142,509 for consulting, creative and production. As the ministry considered our proposal, they had to wrestle with justifying spending this significant sum, since they had historically always done their own fundraising for media needs.

After careful consideration, the ministry decided to take what was for them a risk, and they agreed to our proposal. To their credit, they carefully executed the strategies we recommended without modification. The end result was a record-breaking success of $2.1 million! Not only had their step of faith in spending the $142,509 paid off, but the additional $600,000 raised more than covered our consulting fees. The Return on Investment (ROI) was a very pleasing 14.74/1. They managed the income side of the ledger. There was no guarantee that they would have reached their $1.5 million goal by doing it themselves. Our experience applied to their ministry enabled them to not only replace their analog equipment but purchase some of the items on their wish list to help them continue broadcasting the Good News!

RULE #16

"Income and expense are inextricably linked. It takes money to make money..."

Over the years, I have witnessed many development officers who are caught in, what feels like, the vice-like grips of unrealistic financial expectations. For the development officer it usually begins something like this:

You're meeting with your CEO, CFO and COO, and it's time to balance the annual budget. You've done your job; you've followed the rules and are feeling pretty darn good about the income you and your team have forecasted for the coming year. You've also been very careful to keep your department's expenses to a necessary minimum.

All of the other divisions and departments have submitted their budgets for the year. Of course, they are requesting spending increases and have made very convincing cases for their positions. It's now time to balance the budget.

For you, this can feel a bit like horse-trading meets job security. The CEO is staring at the charts, graphs and spreadsheets all projected on the screen in front of you. The CFO scrolls back and forth between income and expenses. At this point they never match up. No surprises here. It's always this way.

The COO is sitting off to the side, watching the negotiating process that's about to begin. She's not going to jump in too soon. She wants to see how this thing's going to play out for a while.

It's time for the CFO to make his annual pronouncement, "We can't take an unbalanced budget to the board. We never have, and we're not going to start on my watch." The CEO grunts his agreement, but not too loud or too convincingly.

It's too soon for him to show his allegiances. He may not even know what they are as yet.

More scrolling, more sighing, the COO stands up and gets a cup of coffee. She's standing there stirring powdered cow into her Styrofoam cup when she says, "I think we're just going to have to raise more money this year. We've held off on salary increases for two years now and Vision 100 isn't going to happen unless we escalate our efforts."

Now, you know the next person who speaks is going to determine how well this meeting is going to go and how long it's going to last. You want a raise as much as anyone, but you also know the numbers, and they don't support the current $2 million difference between income and expense.

The CFO knows his role. He doesn't want the CEO to have to be the heavy, so he says, "What's it gonna be? Income or expense?" looking back and forth between you and the COO. The COO keeps stirring her coffee, not that it needs it, and you just keep staring at the printed income spreadsheets on the table in front of you. It looks like it's going to be a long meeting...

Now, the titles of the players may be different in your own organization, but the process can't be too far off. Having sat in your chair, I know the drill all too well. The pressures to raise more money are increasing, especially if the economy is less than stellar.

It's quite possible that the solutions to your financial disparity are going to be determined by the personalities of your leadership team, and the strength of your relationships with each other. It comes down to your CEO. What's his personality? Is he aligned more with the COO or you? Is he conflict averse? Or is he just going to make the call? What's his leadership style? Does he empower you, or does he make all the decisions? Only you can answer how this meeting ends. But let me give you a few guidelines:

1. If you have solid relationships with your leadership team, this might be the time to affirm your shared goals and mission. You all want the same things, to reinstate salary increases and escalate efforts so you can achieve Vision 100.

2. You might want to look your CFO in the eyes and acknowledge the financial dilemma you all share.

3. You know you're not going to come out of this thing unscathed, so you might offer some out-of-the-box solutions. After all, it doesn't have to be all or nothing. Perhaps the $2 million can be reduced by reinstating salary increases midyear, if your income supports this action and your expenses are at or below expected levels. This might knock $400,000 off the problem.

4. You offer up one full-time equivalent, by not replacing the person who recently left, with the caveat that you can fill this position when income warrants or if expenses are less than anticipated.

This gives you the reduction of another $70,000 plus benefits.

5. You agree to go back to your team (including your fundraising consulting firm if you have one) and see what it would require to raise an additional $500,000. You've now met the COO halfway; it's her turn.

6. At this point, you may want to just sit back and let your spirit of cooperation work its magic with the rest of the team. Chances are the out-of-the-box thinking will begin a brainstorming session that enables everybody a way out for the remaining $1 million.

I've found that it's in my best interest, and that of my organization, to be the initiator in this process. If I'm not the proactive party, it could result in an artificial income forecast that will be detrimental to all concerned.

Over the years, I have participated in countless meetings where this very scene has been played out. It has never helped me to remain silent and just dig in my heels. Besides, if you're in this situation and have a good fundraising consultant, they'll love the challenge of discovering another strategy to raise the additional half million! It makes them look good and you look good. By keeping your consulting partner in the process, you'll find that you may have resources available to you that may not have considered.

I don't have to tell you about the pressures of being a development officer. You may already know the terrible sense of violation and loss of control that follows someone else taking your carefully crafted income forecast and inadvertently inserting increased financial results. Sadly, I've had this happen to me, and I've seen it done to others more times than I care to remember. I think it's in your best interest to head this kind of action off at the pass. In almost every case I can remember, the original income forecast was indeed correct, unless new strategic thinking and more expenses were allocated. *So, there is an inextricable link between income and expense.* It's a rule that is often broken by those who don't know the rules or choose to ignore them. Yet, all of us know the old adage, "It takes money to make money."

For the board member and CEO so much hinges on the confidence you place in the development officer and her team. If you have established a trust relationship over the years, you would do well to believe the income forecast and expense figures. Working out the issues to close the $2 million gap will still require careful diplomatic and negotiation skills. You may need to consider drawing on cash reserves to supplement some of the income shortfall.

It's important here to determine if the real issue is expense, different strategies or the limitations of your donor base. If your development team has done their job, they have found every donated dollar possible. It may require some outside-the-box thinking like a special campaign to raise the additional $2 million (but this too will require additional resources).

The CEO or Board Member can use this opportunity to express their confidence in the leadership team and diffuse the tension by acknowledging that you know you all share the same goals. This is a time for the leader to lead. Challenge your team by saying something like, "I know we need to do everything in the budget this year. If I can personally raise $1 million, can you use it to fund a matching gift campaign?" It shows your team that you believe the numbers they have prepared and, perhaps even more importantly, that you have skin in the game.

If you are the board member you will need to use your wisdom to help the team determine the cause of the shortfall. If indeed your budget is too aggressive for your pocketbook, you'll need to step in and help them consider a multiyear plan to accomplish the desired growth. If, on the other hand, you and your colleagues on the board have the capacity to give more or, even better, to approach your social peers for this special effort, you will have helped the organization to grow its resource base. It's up to you and the CEO to determine if the development team has done their homework. If you believe them, you should express it and disallow any attempt to increase the income forecast without new strategies and resources. To do otherwise would be devastating to your team and your cause. **Income and expense are inextricably linked, and you may need to help them adhere to this reality.**

RULE #17

"Nobody cares about the details when the money is good... but the details still matter."

It's a fact that CEOs and board members are less inclined to ask questions and drill down into the details of fundraising when the income meets or exceeds expectations. We have a saying at Douglas Shaw & Associates: "It's always more fun to make a visit to a client when the numbers are good."

At the highest levels of an organization, it's the income that matters. This is as it should be. If the mission of your organization is being accomplished and the needed resources are there, then it doesn't matter how the sausage is being made. (Again, assuming the whole moral, ethical and legal thing.) The expense is most often assumed to come within the budget. It's the income that has the most variables, i.e., it may or may not be given by donors as expected, and therefore comes under the most scrutiny, especially when income forecasts are not being met.

Now, there's another shoe, can you hear it dropping? Even though the income is where it needs to be, you still have to have all of the details of your fundraising program up to date. Income needs to be scrutinized just as carefully when the money is at or ahead of your income forecast. This is not an area that can ever be left to occasional updating or inspection on your part. *Not knowing your numbers is tantamount to not caring in the fundraising realm;* and I know you care! This isn't my rule, I wasn't asked for my opinion here, nor was I given a vote.

If you would, let me give you a little shop talk that occurs inside consulting firms. I don't think it's an out-and-out rule, but it comes pretty close. **Don't deluge your board with vast amounts of detail.**

Board reports are why God invented pie charts. Just because you have a laptop or even a 4-inch binder filled with analytics doesn't mean your board should ever be allowed to delve into this treasure trove. My apologies in advance to board members here, but I've made this mistake, and before I knew it the bean counters of the world took over and began managing my fundraising department for me. It's

not a pleasant experience to have the board treasurer making direct mail segmentation decisions; they may know accounting, but they certainly don't know the rules of raising
money.

By carefully monitoring your income and expenses on
a consistent basis it will demonstrate to your ministry's
leadership that you are at the top of your game. But perhaps equally important, monitoring your numbers when
income is strong allows you to make decisions that will prevent you from leaving money on the table. This is how financial breakthroughs occur. Spot something that's
working and do more of it! For example, a few years ago we
were serving a well-known radio ministry and our appeals
were not generating the response we had forecast.

We knew we needed to give their development program a jump-start, so we decided to develop what we now
call a Major Donor Proposal appeal (this is described in detail at the end of Rule #10). We mailed to the top 2,500 donors of this ministry and grossed over $639,000! The cost,
$29,000, was insignificant by comparison. This approach
quickly became a regular part of their annual fundraising
plan. We have since used this approach for many organizations with extremely satisfying results. Now you can use it
too!

Conversely, knowing that you're not going to achieve your income forecast on a specific effort can be an opportunity as well. The sooner you know the money is falling short, the sooner you can take corrective action. This is the reason we have developed a special report for the nonprofits we serve that helps us to know after only **nine days** whether or not a direct mail appeal will achieve its forecast. We call it a "Days Out Report." Based on your organization's day-by-day historic income flow from an appeal letter, a predictive model can be built to give you an early warning signal when it appears that the response to an appeal feels soft.

How does this create opportunity? Well, when you know a specific topic or "offer" doesn't do what is expected it allows for you to take corrective action. For example, let's say your report indicates that you are going to miss your forecast by 30% or $50,000. By seeing this coming at you more quickly, you can create calling campaigns, e-mail blast follow-ups or place a special stuffer in all of your receipt packages to strengthen your receipt income. You may also decide to place a cover note in the package containing your next newsletter that tells your donors that giving has been soft and you need any extra help they can give right now.

To summarize, knowing what works allows you to do more of it. And knowing what doesn't work provides you with quick information to adjust your funding strategies in order to take corrective action. Watching the details, even when the income is solid, can create opportunities to adjust upcoming efforts and provide more income for your cause.

RULE #18

"A good idea is always in the budget."

You've heard me carry on ad nauseam about not liking rules. Well…so much for being consistent, actually I kind of like this one. I like it because it rewards proven strategies that can be supported with documented results.

It's early in the history of Douglas Shaw & Associates, before we had real offices, and I'm sitting at my desk in the town Doctor's Residence of Wheaton, Illinois. The 1880s building hasn't been occupied by the family for many years. The old medicine man has been gone for some time now. I believe my "office" used to be one of his guest rooms. It now has a glorious view of the parking lot of the Gary United Methodist Church next door. I'm sitting here thinking that I need to come up with another, new-to-me, proven strategy that will benefit the nonprofits that I'm serving. I mentally tick off what's been working:

- Matching Gift offers
- Certificates of Appreciation
- Emergency Grams (when there's a legitimate emergency)

I can think of a few others too, but I need something really new and different that will make donors sit up, take notice and above all—give! I'm quickly approaching the fundraising consultant's equivalent to writer's block. Searching my mental Rolodex (it's an old-fashioned, paper-based system for storing names and contact information), I decide to call a friend who is the vice president of development for a highly successful and continually growing organization in Seattle. Thankfully Jenny's there, and she takes my call.

"Doug, how are you?" she says enthusiastically. "Well Jenny...I'm stuck! I need a great fundraising idea that blows the doors off! Would you mind telling me what your most successful strategy is—you know, the best idea you've used in the last couple of years?" Jenny responds without hesitation, "You're using a handwritten appeal, aren't you?" "Uh," I say, "I've heard of them, but I don't have any hard evidence that they work." "Oh, man!" Jenny becomes even more enthusiastic, "I've mailed this thing five times now, and it beats anything else I've ever done!" I sit up straight in my chair now. "Really?" I say hopefully, "Would you mind sharing your strategy?" "I can do better than that," she replies, "I can send you the package and the results too! In fact, I'll fax you the results right after we get off the phone." "Jenny! You're a godsend! Can I ask you one more favor?" "Go for it!" she offers. "Could I share your results with other organizations like yours?" Without hesitation she says, "Absolutely! We're all regional so we're not in competition. I'm glad to help anyone else who's helping the homeless!"

Jenny's an absolute delight! We catch up with each other for a couple of minutes, say our goodbyes, and I race for the fax. True to her word, within five minutes I'm holding hard evidence for the performance of Jenny's handwritten direct mail appeals. I can't believe what I'm reading. These are some of the best results I've ever seen! Walking back to my desk I sit down and study them line by line. I'm jubilant, but my ego is moving in quickly to try and spoil the moment. "Why haven't I thought of this?" I ask myself. I must not be a very good consultant. Nope. Stop it! This isn't the time for bouncing my head off the top of my desk. The idea's been around for a long time. It's just that I didn't have the data I needed to confidently recommend it to my clients. "Okay, okay calm yourself down," I coax. Boy I can't wait to get my hands on the package itself. A few days later it arrives...

It's so simple! I'm shocked at how basic this package is. It's expensive though, because it requires personal hand-writing and a 1st class stamp. The cost for Jenny's package is $1.26 each, in 1998 dollars. But the return is fantastic! In some cases she's raised $10 for every $1 spent.

I decide to bring this idea to my oldest and largest client. They, after all, have been very generous in allowing me to share their successes with other homeless causes. It feels great to be able to bring a highly successful idea to them.

Now, homeless shelters are not known for being willing to spend very much money on fundraising. They tend to be extremely frugal. I know the challenge that lies before me will be to overcome their culture of frugality.

The day arrives for our meeting in Houston. As we sit together I can't wait to get this on the table. It's the first item on the agenda. I begin with the presentation of the package. The development team studies it carefully. It's quiet. "Too simple," I think. Now it's time for the show! I slowly and dra-matically slide the printed reports across the table to each of them. I'm studying their faces for response. The Vice President's eyebrows fly up, "Really?" she asks. I sit there like a proud father showing the latest photos of little Ralphie. "Yes, and they've used it five times in two years with the amazing results you have in front of you." I now brace myself for the expense conversation. To my surprise it doesn't come!

"Would you like to test this idea for August? We all know it's the worst performing month of the year," I say. "Yeah," someone says mournfully. "In Houston, anyone with any money or sense leaves town during the month of August."

The Vice President mulls my question over, but just for a few seconds, then she looks up and answers, "What've we got to lose? Nothing we've ever tried in August really works. Let's roll it out!" This surprises me, so I ask one more question; "What about the price?" "We'll find the money," she says with determination. It was the best August we'd ever seen!

Now, friends with proven ideas, like Jenny, are hard to find. I realize not everyone has a trusted colleague in a similar market who can or will send you detailed results and direct mail packages; no one to direct you to a website or send you send you to their latest podcast using their best on-air offer. So what do you do when you've got a great idea and want to try it, but you have little or no data to prove it will work? So much of what could be done depends upon your knowledge of the Rules of Fundraising.

This is where the old saying, "A little knowledge is a dangerous thing," comes into play. If you're a veteran fundraiser and have years of rule-following under your belt you might want to go ahead, press the envelope. If you're a beginner, or only a few years into negotiating the foothills of philanthropy, you may want to proceed with a little more caution. Test the idea without betting the farm.

Since we're considering the rule, "A good idea is always in the budget," let's take a moment to look at a few of the classic idea-killers. Here are some of the most amazingly paralyzing phrases in the world of philanthropy:

1. *"We've never done it this way before."* So? How is a fundraiser going to break new ground without trying new ideas? If memory serves, the definition of insanity is "doing the same thing over and over and expecting different results." I've found that life itself is a risk; if I applied idea-killer #1 to my everyday life I'd still be pumping gas in Ellensburg, Washington, instead of finishing college and graduate school. I was scared to venture out of my safety zone, but at least I tried!

2. *"We don't have it in our budget."* To my way of thinking, this is the very essence of this rule: Great ideas are always in the budget. It never ceases to amaze me how flexible management and boards can be when it comes to investing resources in truly great ideas. Budgets exist to be modified if the circumstances change. If we are unwilling to ask for a budget modification then we'll likely succumb to the paralysis of inside-the-box thinking.

3. *"The boss will never buy this idea."* How do we know if we don't ask? We're not mind readers after all. Most leaders are inspired by people who are willing to risk raising questions and speaking their minds. If your leader is not, then you probably are going to want to invoke the 18-month clause in development life and find a new position where thinking is rewarded.

4. *"That's not the way we do things around here."* This is tantamount to saying, "We invent our own rules!" I'm afraid, very, very afraid, of this well-used idea-killer. It's the kind of thinking that makes me start considering going to the nearest Office Depot to look for moving boxes for the cluttered contents of my desk.

5. *"I don't like it."* So? I don't like paying taxes either, but I do it anyway. It's a choice after all. I can pay my taxes or

go directly to jail, without passing GO or collecting $200. Most often this idea-killer is simply an expression of "My thinking is better than yours," or another way of saying this is, "If it's not invented here, it's not worth doing." If I encounter this kind of thinking on a regular basis it's moving box time. There are too many other great causes to work for that are eager for great thinking.

6. *"That's a stupid idea."* My advice to you here is to flee as quickly as you can! Don't even stop to clean out your desk, just grab your purse or wallet and get out of the building as quickly as your feet can carry you! This kind of thinking is a judgmental statement that roughly translates into, "I know everything, and you don't know anything." Run! Your self-esteem and reputation are in great danger!

7. *"I've tried that in the past and it doesn't work."* This idea-killer is usually used as the ultimate trump card for someone who may have tried something *similar* in the past but didn't know the rules or chose to ignore them. Only the facts can be used to refute the "reality" in this person's world. I've found that this response requires a lot of digging around in the archives to be able to examine the evidence. If you find the rules were followed, then maybe they have a point. However, it's usually

been my experience that there was a flaw somewhere. The dicey part is reapproaching the boss carefully and humbly, so she/he is not threatened by what you've found. This can be made easier by giving credit where credit is due. Phrases like, "I think you were on to something when you tried this idea. I did a little digging, and I think I may have found an insight that can make your idea into what you were hoping when you tried it before."

You might want to comfort yourself with this thought; good ideas change the world. A great idea can totally revolutionize your ability to fulfill your mission. I've found it's usually worth the effort to build my case with as many tangible examples and facts as possible. If my great idea still isn't accepted, I'll save it for a rainy day. When the umbrellas come out and the waters begin to rise, it's amazing how rejected ideas seem worth reconsidering.

Let me revisit idea-killer #5, "I don't like it." A few years ago we were trying to sell an organization our services.

The CEO was listening to our presentation and nodding approvingly...at least until we brought up the idea of using direct mail to acquire new donors for his cause. At the first mention of this concept, he visibly stiffened, turned red in the face and said, "You were doing great until now!" My great powers of perception kicked in, and I realized he didn't like what we were saying.

It's one of the conundrums of consulting; you know an organization will benefit from a specific strategy, but they just won't let you try it. It didn't take a genius to know it was time to drop the subject...for now. A few days later we were hired to represent this excellent nonprofit, and we dug right in. A few weeks later, the development officer called one of our consultants and asked, "How much money are we giving up by not doing direct mail donor acquisition?" Our consultant pulled out our proposal and read, "Oh, about $3.5 million over the next six years." The development officer replied, "Help me put together a flow chart of income, and I'll take it to the boss." When the CEO saw that his refusal to use our recommended approach was going to cost his company such significant income he quickly changed his mind. By the way, when we finally executed our plan to acquire new donors the results surpassed even our expectations! Even idea-killers can be overcome when it's a proven idea.

That's why a good idea is always in the budget!

RULE #19

"You don't have to guess!"

I've found that the earlier we, as fundraisers, learn this rule, the more likely we are to have more successful, fulfilling and lengthy careers. By guessing, I'm referring to the innate desire or need we all have to rely on our instincts or memory when it comes to the reality of fundraising. It usually plays out something like this, "How many hits did we get on our website last month?" Rather than turning on our computer and using the measurement tools we've purchased, we guess, "Oh, about 30,000, I think." Of the countless guesses I've made over the last 30 years, about two were correct. So, when I've asked development officers to have this information verified, I have learned to brace myself for the inevitable look that communicates, "So, you think I don't know my own numbers?" "Oh, I'm sure you're right," I offer, "But we're about to make some significant decisions based on this information, so would you mind verifying the number?" A phone call is made, some I.T. person comes scrambling up the stairs, out of breath, sits down at her laptop and makes an inquiry. "Let's see here, it looks like we've had 3,000 hits during the last month." "Oh, yeah, that's right! I was thinking about the number of hits in the last 10 months!" the fundraising officer suddenly remembers. Like I say, I've done this same thing many times and encountered the limits of my memory more times than not (but I'm usually not off by more than a few decimal points).

If I could make up a rule, which of course we know I cannot, I'd make a rule that says, "In order to be a fundraiser, or fundraising consultant, you must wear a tattoo on your right wrist that simply reads, 'You don't have to guess!'" (Tattoo colors and accompanying artwork choices would be left to the style preferences, generation and wardrobe of the fundraiser, of course.)

There are few things that I'm absolutely fanatical about, but getting accurate, up-to-date information and metrics before making decisions is one of them.

I was talking to my friend Wiley Stinnett again the other day, and he added this little dab of wisdom to our discussion: "If you can't measure it, it shouldn't be done." He's right about 99% of the time, so I'd listen to him if I were you. Since measurement can only be conducted by studying hard data, it means we must have everything measured and available when we need it. The only caveat I would add is that we are talking about fundraising here. This is not a universal rule for all disciplines.

Now I know full well that this rule can make the public relations department a little nervous. But that need not be the case. Solid PR efforts will undoubtedly cause overall income to increase. It's most often seen in the influx of new, unsolicited gifts (what many of us have come to know as "white mail" because it arrives in an unmarked white envelope and can't be traced to any other source) or when online donations take an uncharacteristic jump.

As you know, in development, there are a lot of great opportunities that come our way. One of my greatest challenges has been to sort out the productive ideas or opportunities from the unproductive. It seems that what I let go of is just as important as what I hang on to.

One day a client called me in a very excited state. A friend of their organization had just called them to tell them that they were going to hold a concert at The Dorothy Chandler Pavilion in Los Angeles. All of the proceeds from this concert, after covering the direct costs, were going directly to help this organization. My antenna flew up like the guy in My Favorite Martian (an old black and white TV series I watched as a kid; Google it if you need to).

"Ah," I said hesitantly. "Who is this person? Are they a recognized artist?" It turned out this generous friend was a vocalist of questionable talent and had always dreamed of playing this venue.

Now I'm leaning forward in my chair and beginning to scratch my forehead; a few wisps of hair fall out. "What's this artist's name?" I inquired. It was somebody I had never heard of. As the story unfolded, it seems this artist wasn't known by anybody. She just wanted to have a huge stage with spotlights shining down on her and throngs of adoring fans screaming her name. The only thing this organization had to do was to sell all the tickets! "Oh boy," I exclaimed, "That's the hardest part!" Thankfully there's a happy ending to this story...upon looking carefully at the reality of the situation, the organization graciously declined this generous offer but assured the vocalist that they would be delighted to be the beneficiary of any excess funding generated by her concert; they just weren't in a position to sell tickets. Nothing ever came of it.

Years ago, while driving and listening to the radio, I heard a news story that made me sit up and take notice.

According to the newscaster, Frank Sinatra had just performed a benefit concert in Lake Tahoe. It was for a great cause, and the evening involved the raffling off of a beautiful, brand-spanking-new red Porsche 911. The evening was a great success, a good time was had by all and a total of $16,000 had been raised for this wonderful charity. "What?" I said to myself. "The car cost more than that! Why didn't they just sell the car and give the money to charity?" I can't imagine the days, weeks and months of planning that may have gone into setting up the benefit concert. I hope somebody got the Chairman of the Board's autograph...maybe they could sell it later.

Now, I know the circumstances of the unknown vocalist, she was primarily interested in having someone sell tickets for her dream performance. She wasn't making a gift; she was trying to receive one. Except we caught on and decided to graciously extricate the organization from weeks or months of hard, distracting work followed by an evening of embarrassment.

In the case of the Lake Tahoe event I can only speculate. My first thought was, "Ol' Blue Eyes figured out a way to have a party for his friends and not pay for it." But this doesn't hold up under scrutiny. Frank Sinatra could have bought the place had he wanted to. Saving a few thousand dollars on a party would not have been much of a motivation. More likely it all started off with good intentions.

Somebody probably wanted to give their major donors a good time and build closer relationships with them. They may have also wanted to be able to tell their friends at the next meeting of the Association of Fundraising Professionals (AFP) that they had met Frank Sinatra and had their picture taken too! Porsche had been generous and donated the 911! Or did they? I'm still wondering about this.

The more I think about the Lake Tahoe event, it seems like everyone got their money's worth except the organization who must have invested inordinate amounts of time planning the event.

This rule is here for a time-tested reason. As a charitable cause you exist to fulfill your mission. But, sad as it is, there are people out there who will use your good name and cause to further their own agenda. Establishing the metrics of an "opportunity," ahead of time, can prevent the distracting loss of precious time that development officers and their employing organizations seem to always find in short supply.

That's how we avoided the Dorothy Chandler Pavilion disaster. We obtained the figures for the cost of the evening and realized it would not have broken even, let alone raised money for the charity.

Those who have honed their development skills know that measuring everything is critical in fundraising. As you continue to build your own guidebook of rules and all the metrics of fundraising, you'll become far more adept at spotting opportunities that you will want to pass by. Using your experience and growing supply of information will allow you to utilize the data to forecast the likely outcome of any opportunity. One of our clients, who happens to have had a long career in engineering, likes to say, "Bad data makes poor choices." If your experience is anything like mine, you know that guessing most often results in bad data.

RULE #20

"Test, test, test!"

"Testing" is one of a journeyman fundraiser's favorite words. I salivate at the mere mention of testing. It's not particularly profound to mention that there are already enough risks in life; so the many unknowns inherent in fundraising can become much more palatable when testing is an option.

Testing a concept, package, approach, offer, message, channel, gift amounts or a myriad of strategic options allows you to verify your assumptions or disprove your beliefs. It turns speculation into solid, verifiable information. It creates the platform for reality that can then support any development program. Without testing, we're just guessing, and, to put things bluntly, being imprudent.

None of us are in this great world of philanthropy for the money or prestige it provides. We're here because we feel "called", and we care. Testing will strengthen your ability to thoughtfully fund the cause you've given your life to promote.

After blowing it countless times, I've finally figured out there are many variables involved in conducting valid tests. As one fundraiser to another I urge great caution here. Here's an example of a valid test:

TEST #1

A nonprofit we serve wanted to know if printing their two- color newsletter in four colors would result in significantly more income. We thought so but couldn't say for sure, so we decided it was worth a test. Here's what we did:

1. We tested only one variable so we would know that the change in the colors either generated more income, less income or the same amount. We also wanted to know if donors would react negatively to the organization's spending their donations using four colors (there was concern that it might look too expensive).

2. We conducted an Nth name select of our donors. It took me a while to learn what this meant. I found out that all this means is we used a random data selection technique, so every name had an equal chance of being placed in panel A: four color or panel B: two color. We didn't want to bias the results by just using every other name for each panel. We ended up with approximately 26,000 active donors in each panel.

3. All other variables remained exactly the same between the two panels: stories, photos, carrier envelopes, reply envelopes, reply devices, eight pages and mail dates.

The only difference was Panel A was a four-color newsletter and Panel B was a two-color newsletter. Again, the content (photos and copy) for both were exactly the same.

This was a great test, meaning the results were conclusive. And there were no donor complaints!

THE RESULTS:

- Panel A: Four-color results: $54,000 (these responses had one large gift of $17,000, so we factored it out of the results)
- Panel B: Two-color results: $11,500 (with no large gifts)

I remember asking my client if they wanted to test this approach again to further prove the results. I've found that it's usually a good idea to conduct multiple tests, just in case the results were impacted by a variable that we had not yet discovered. But the VP of development said, "No, I'm not willing to give up the money to find out." So, we stayed with the four-color newsletter. The results have remained consistently higher than what we were experiencing with two-color newsletters.

The incremental costs associated with the four-color approach were more than recovered.

TEST #2

Not long ago, a media ministry we serve instructed us to do a "test" for them. Only it wasn't a valid test. The results were skewed from the start by having more than one variable. Our recommendations to make the test legitimate were indisputably overruled. This pseudo-test required the following:

1. All donor file names with e-mail addresses were to be sent an e-mail version of a direct mail package we had developed for them. There was no Nth name

select, everyone with an e-mail address was selected.

2. The second panel of this pseudo-test was for all remaining donors who did NOT have an e-mail address. The direct mail package was snail-mailed to
them.

THE RESULTS:

- Panel A: E-mail $2,400 after 30 days
- Panel B: Snail-Mail $24,000 after 30 days

Believe it or not, this was NOT a successful test. The
broadcast ministry was hoping to eliminate the expense of
snail-mail by proving that e-mail would raise just as much
income as snail-mail at a fraction of the cost.

Even if the results had been reversed, this pseudo-test
would not have proven the point. By selecting ALL donor
names with e-mail addresses biased the data, most likely in
favor of the client-desired outcome. It would have been a
very dangerous thing for this pseudo-test to have proven
what the organization was hoping for. If you're wondering
why this would have been dangerous, which is a completely
understandable question, it's because of what the nonprofit was planning to do with the outcome of the test. Had

the online panel outperformed the snail-mail panel, the broadcaster was planning on scrapping or greatly diminishing its use of snail-mail, which would have been much to their detriment.

This is a true example of rolling the dice. The end result was a loss of $21,600, if we can assume the e-mail responders would have performed at the same level as the snail-mail folks had they received a direct mail appeal. Quite unintentionally, this was not a wise use of donor dollars. Equally as important, several other rules were broken in this effort that, if not adhered to in the future, will negatively impact the effectiveness of this great cause. There's a country saying that I like a lot, "Don't hire a dog and then bark yourself!" It's a wonderfully rural way of saying, "If you're going to hire a consultant, listen to them!"

If you are a seasoned fundraising professional, you know that a well-designed test can provide invaluable information that can propel your organization forward. But even in this pseudo-test there was a lesson to be learned...valid testing is how you begin to learn more about the rules!

One last thought about testing. Having my intuition proven right is not where I've gained the most insight. Testing, for me, is about determining what is real, i.e., what works, what raises the most money for your cause. I have often learned more from having a test prove my intuition wrong than confirm that I was right. That's why I continue in my commitment to test, test, test.

RULE #21

"You must track your results, review them thoroughly and act upon them thoughtfully."

It might be too strong to say, "The very existence of your ministry, cause or organization is dependent upon you learning and living by this rule." As fundraisers we have enough anxiety as it is. It feels like I often run around like a complete lunatic with what seems to be the world's most important questions swirling through my brain.

Well, I've found that, for me, ignoring this rule will cause more anxiety than following it. I admit a certain amount of neurosis when it comes to knowing the yield of my efforts.

I've been known to stand in the accounting department anxiously awaiting the day's donation tally (I can hear you laughing, but you've probably done it too). But there's hope for the neurotic in all of us, and sometimes it comes from unlikely places, like Ecclesiastes:

> *"Who is like a wise man? And who knows the*
> *interpretation of a thing? A man's wisdom*
> *makes his face shine, And the sternness of his*
> *face is changed."*
> *Ecclesiastes 8:1-3, NKJV*

In a very real sense, we hold the health of our organizations in our minds, by what we measure and by what we do with what we learn. Perhaps even more important is what we choose to track or measure.

Most CFOs will tell you that expenses are real. That money will be spent is certain, but income is elusive; it may not come in as planned. Generally, accountants have concrete perspectives. Money is either revenue or an expense. As I've mentioned, there are Generally Accepted Rules for accounting. In fact, the IRS looks to the accountants of the world for truth and accountability, not us fundraisers. So we will do well to follow their example on this one.

The fundraising industry, or community, has no legal entity or ironclad standard to hold us accountable; therefore, we have to create our own. In the past few decades groups like Charity Navigator and The Evangelical Council for Financial Accountability (ECFA) have emerged just for this reason; to help donors be informed of which organizations are fiscally sound. But even here, they rely on accounting ratios to rate the efficiencies of charities. The loss of a single star on a five-star rating system can wreak havoc in boards, development committees and leadership teams, and this havoc filters down to us and our development teams. So it all really comes back to us. Either we track, think and respond to carefully compiled income figures, or someone else will do it for us.

And they seldom know the Rules of Fundraising; that's why I've found that it's just good sense that we know and follow the rules, including this one.

In order to track fundraising results with any degree of accuracy, we need codes. I'm not thinking of a "code of ethics" here; I mean, quite literally, some kind of numeric or alphanumeric codes that allow us to track every single element of every single fundraising effort; e.g., A12601 might simply mean A=appeal, 1=January, 26=year and 01=segment 1, which could be donors giving $1,000 or more. I often find myself saying to clients, "Codes are free! Use them liberally. Code everything that wiggles!" This allows us to carefully track results and respond thoughtfully. In addition to the code above, you will want to also have your donor's identification number on everything you mail to them.

I have, on occasion, been absolutely devastated after launching a critical fundraising effort only to find out that the data entry person or department didn't know to enter the codes along with the amount of the gifts. Believe it or not, I've actually had people tell me that they didn't enter the "motivation" or "source" codes because they didn't want to have to use the extra keystrokes—because it slowed them down! I'm not exaggerating here. This is a common problem, especially with smaller organizations. I think this must be why I'm bald!

Larger not-for-profit organizations devote entire departments to data entry. They know this is key to their knowledge and therefore to their financial health. The really astute organizations have placed the data entry departments inside or under the supervision of the development department. Who is going to know more about attributing donations and coding than experienced fundraisers?

The way I've experienced it, direct mail fundraising requires more codes and data entry than just about any other development effort. Even in smaller organizations a single mailing can have scores if not hundreds of segments and codes. But please, be gentle with me now. I didn't make this rule, I'm just letting you know that it exists. So, please don't shoot the messenger.

I may not like all the hassles of coding, but, I must confess here, I absolutely love the end result of quality tracking; it's extremely rewarding. It provides me with the critical information I need to make thoughtful decisions. In defense of coding everything, it might be helpful to keep this in mind: We can always compile coded gifts into summary form, but we can never accurately split apart large groups of information into meaningful segments after the fact.

Now for the second part of this tedious yet important rule: "Review the results thoroughly." Just about all development software packages have some form of reporting components. Some will work off-the-shelf, like Raiser's Edge™ from Blackbaud®, DonorDirect™, Virtuous™ or Fundraise Up™, while others may require exporting data into Excel™, or some other software. Whatever it takes, it needs to be done in order for us to give thorough review to our development efforts. I know this may seem like a difficult thing to do. But we have a saying at Douglas Shaw & Associates: "If it were easy, anybody could do it."

I remember spending one entire Christmas holiday sorting through a client's direct mail reply devices. It was when we'd first started our company, and we were still operating out of our basement. I had these little green buck-slip (8-½ X 3-½ inch) reply devices spread out all over our carpet. The nonprofit didn't have enough staff to sort through all of the comments we'd solicited from donors, so I did it. As sick as it sounds, I found it exhilarating! There, written in ink, were donors' comments on what they liked best about the organization. It touched me deeply to realize just how much people were benefiting from the services this group offered. Most of the handwritten notes were from elderly people, so I found myself squinting, trying to make sense out of the shaky lines that communicated the heartfelt messages the donors had taken the time to write. The process was tedious but heartwarming and inspiring. One note in particular stands out in my memory. I read how two sisters had been estranged for 50 years!

This organization had helped them with their conflict and true feelings for each other, and the scribbled note was a celebration of two women who could now spend their remaining years laughing, talking and loving each other again. They had miraculously renewed their relationship.

If I hadn't taken the time to dig into the stacks and stacks of donor comments, I would never have discovered this wonderful story of changed lives.

We used this incredible story in an appeal letter to further support this great organization.

So, it probably goes without saying, but...I'm going to say it anyway: Reports and donor feedback need to be gathered, reviewed and acted upon with great regularity. Just as in accounting, no month should pass without reviewing the work of our hearts, hands and minds.

Results are our monthly report card. But more importantly, a thorough review will tell us what is working, how well it's working and what would work better if we tested or adjusted our strategies. It will also tell us what strategies to abandon.

It's this information that will help us to reallocate our resources in order to maximize our fundraising efforts.

The third portion of this rule is, "acting thoughtfully." Up until now we have moved the ball a little, gathered and reviewed information. But the ball needs to keep moving, and in the right direction. This won't happen until we "execute" based upon what we've learned.

Enter the ego! What if an idea we sold to our supervisor didn't work? And to make matters worse, what if she told us she thought the approach was "highly questionable"? This is when we earn our stripes as fundraisers. I've found that sweeping bad news under the carpet won't help. For me, this is, as I have said before, when I have to step back, take a deep breath and begin unbuckling the buttons and belts of my psychological defenses. This is when I say to myself, "Go ahead, slide your ego gently to the ground and allow your defenselessness to be completely seen in its entirety." Just know that if you ever encounter a moment like this, you're officially joining the ranks of the fundraising craftsman! In truth, we've all been here. This is one of the ways we've learned the rules, by running the gauntlet of failure.

Today, "running the gauntlet" has become a common phrase for anyone who has to go through a period of judgment or exhausting evaluation. I've been there, when I served in a nonprofit, sitting in a leadership team meeting, among my peers and supervisor. All eyes turn on me when the income is not coming in as is planned. At the very least, I'm expected to know my numbers. It's better if I know the reasons for the lack of income. But it's best if I know how to turn the circumstances around and release those in the spending part of the organization to go back to their work, without worry. For most causes, thoughtful action is the only acceptable answer. Owning this rule is at the very heart of fundraising. Admitting that we don't have the answer requires humility, courage and a very thick skin. I've left meetings of this sort, withdrawn to my office and kicked the trash can!

It's what we do after the initial tears have dried that counts. Moving the ball means getting back into the game even after having our best moves go unrewarded. When our hearts are broken by our own inability to provide the money our cause needs and deserves, it is a true test of our personal character, self-confidence and faith.

If we have measured "everything that wiggles" we'll have a solid place to begin fixing our income problems. That's why we track our results, review them thoroughly and act upon them thoughtfully.

RULE #22

"There is no well to run dry; there's only a river to pass you by."

You've heard it; I know certainly I have, more times than I can count. It usually pops out of somebody's mouth when the topic of the appropriate number of times to mail fundraising appeals is on the table. It usually slips through the lips like this: "We don't want to go to the well too often."

Remember the film, The Matrix? There's a surreal scene where a little bald boy, resembling some kind of monk, holds up a spoon and bends it with his mind powers. Then he says, in a distant sort of trancelike state, "There is no spoon." I admit, this is a little weird even for me. But in the case of fundraising...there is no well!

Many nonprofit executives, and sometimes development officers too, have the image of the well in their minds when they think of donor giving. It's like there is some sort of container with a limited amount of funding in it out there, and we have to be careful not to drain it!

One of my employees made this point to me a few years ago: "Funding sources are more like rivers, not wells." In reality, funding sources or "rivers," if you will, flow past you every day. The river doesn't just turn on and off, and it never runs dry. People give out of their discretionary income. They pay their bills, save for retirement and then give to causes they believe in. That's the good news. The bad news is the riverbanks are crowded with fishermen. Everybody and his sister has a line in the water.

You need to be in regular contact with donors that give to you. One good reason for frequent contact is you'll generate more goodwill and income. Another good reason is if you aren't in front of the donor, others will be. Now I've heard all of the platitudes about fundraising not being a competition. I'm not so sure I believe this line of thinking. We may not like to think of our nonprofit work as competitive, but in my experience, it is.

Again, I didn't get a vote on this. It just is.

So, when you sit down to determine how frequently you should make appeals to your donors, you might be better served thinking of a river rather than a well. Most organizations we serve mail between 12 and 15 direct mail appeals a year. If this makes you uncomfortable, that's okay. A little discomfort goes a long way when increasing the income for your cause is at stake. In addition to direct mail appeals, most organizations we serve also mail income-producing newsletters 4-6 times a year. If you're new to direct response fundraising, this might put a knot in your throat, or maybe someplace else. But it is a reality, at least here in the States.

But let's talk for a moment about the many organizations that are mailing appeals to donors 2-4 times per year. Jumping right into a full stream of 12-15 appeals and 4-6 newsletters may not be the most prudent approach. I risk being accused of inconsistency here, I realize, but hey, what else is new. This is fundraising, and it has its own rules. If you are mailing 2-4 appeals per year, you may want to ramp up your frequency to 6 appeals and 4 newsletters in your first year, add another appeal or two in the second year and then go flat out in year three.

This gives donors the opportunity to adjust to your frequency of communication. After all, it's about them, not us.

If you're really strapped for cash and are flirting with the idea of going to a full mailing schedule in year one, you do have an option. When complaints about too much mail come in, and they will, you can turn this into an opportunity for donor contact and goodwill.

When a donor contacts you complaining about receiving too much mail, I wouldn't recommend sending them yet another piece of mail telling them that you've heard them. People do this, I'm serious! Here's an approach for your consideration:

1. Pick up the phone and call them
2. Thank them for making their contact preferences known
3. Don't ask them how often they want to receive mailings (you either won't like the answer or they won't know what the options are)
4. Rather, offer them a menu. Here's a little script that might help:

   "Thanks for letting us know that you are receiving too much mail. We are just calling to let you know that we've heard you. This is not a call to request more funds."

   Pause for their response.

   "We are mailing more frequently because the friends of our organization want to be better informed about

what their gifts are accomplishing. Also, we actually receive many more gifts by communicating more frequently. But since you've indicated that you would like to receive fewer mailings, I'd like to ask you your opinion if that's okay."

Pause for their response.

"Some donors like to hear from us monthly, others prefer every other month, some like to hear from us quarterly. Do you have a preference?"

Pause for their response.

"Thank you for taking the time to tell me your thinking on this. I promise we'll change the number of mailings you receive according to your wishes."

I believe that what you do next is extremely important. You might want to check and see if this donor is scheduled to receive the next appeal. If they are, and have requested fewer appeals, suppress their name from this one and code them to receive appeals according to their wishes. I've actually been known to dig through several boxes of outgoing mail to retrieve a donor's mailing piece so I can keep my promise to them.

Now here's something that may surprise you, I know it did me when I first made calls of this kind: Most donors are quite pleased that you have taken the time to call them and discuss their preferences.

The most common response to the menu outlined above is: "Well, that's okay, you can leave it the way it is!" It's counter-intuitive, isn't it?

There is no well to run dry, but there is a river, and you get to fish in it as often as you need to and your donors allow.

RULE #23

"Acquiring new donors is a continuous process and NEVER optional."

The Western Coast of Vancouver Island, in British Columbia, is so beautiful that early navigators couldn't resist sailing up to the coastline. The pounding surf, the tall cedars and the smell of the wild spun a trance that early sea captains simply could not resist. Setting their course for shore, they found it to be not only beautiful, but one of the most dangerous places in the world to navigate.

Hundreds of wooden sailing ships were lost to the submerged rocks in this idyllic setting, so many in fact, that it still, to this day, known as the Graveyard of the Pacific! This is donor acquisition! More money has been unintentionally lost on this critical aspect of fundraising than, perhaps, any other effort.

Acquiring new donors is a continuous process and NEVER optional. In other words, we HAVE to sail into the shore, and we have to do it again and again. That's the rule, and we can only follow it.

If we decide to turn our vessels around and flee the danger we'll never be able to help the cause we've sworn to protect, preserve and grow.

So how do we navigate these rocky waters? Most organizations have found it necessary to hire an experienced guide in order to safely arrive at their destination. (We've already talked about how to select help when you need it.) When I first began my adventures into the risky world of acquiring new donors, I felt lost, alone and in great danger of making a mistake that could cost my organization hundreds of thousands of donated dollars.

The fear that usually accompanies launching into donor acquisition is not only common, but well deserved. This is one of the most difficult aspects of fundraising, requiring exceptional knowledge of a special set of rules and variables.

There are not only special rules governing donor acquisition; there is a special language as well. Now, I have a confession to make here. I was kicked out of high school French (for misbehavior), and I got a D- in Spanish. But on the upside, I did pass three years of Greek in college and tested out of Greek in seminary. So I am much better in languages where pronunciation doesn't count. With this little bit of personal history in mind let's see how I do in explaining the language of donor acquisition.

DONOR ACQUISITION:

This is the acquiring of new donors for your cause. This means you contact a prospect with a message that results in their giving you a gift. This is 1-step marketing in that 1 effort results in a giving transaction.

NAME ACQUISITION:

This is the acquiring of new names, not donors, who can then be cultivated into a donor relationship. This is generally used only in circumstances where you have attempted donor acquisition and it hasn't been successful. This is 2-step marketing in that the 1st step is to get someone to respond to you by sending you their qualified name. The 2nd step is the cultivation process that results in the new name becoming a new donor. This process is longer and more costly than donor acquisition. But in many cases, this is the only option open to a nonprofit (especially if you have a more cerebral rather than emotional mission).

A PROSPECT:

Is a person whom you have identified as a likely candidate to become a donor through gender, age, income or many other traits that are shared by your existing donors.

RENTAL LISTS:

These are lists available to rent on a one-time basis. This is done on the honor system. Should you decide to keep the list and, without permission, continue to use it for acquisition purposes, you will be barred from renting lists in the future. Most list rental companies, or list brokers, "seed" the lists you rent, with their own names, to monitor your usage. There are many types of lists available for rental:

1. *Response lists:* Are lists of the names of people who have responded to other organizations or "offers" (like in Rule #8, the 5 Commandments). These people have proven their direct mail responsiveness through past actions. While more expensive to rent, these lists are generally considered most desirable for response, hence their name.

2. *Compiled lists:* Are lists of names that have been compiled from several sources. They have not

necessarily proven their responsiveness to direct mail fundraising offers. Their primary value comes in the ability to rent large numbers of names based upon criteria like age, income, gender, etc. These lists are less expensive to rent because they do not produce at the same level as response lists.

3. *Saturation lists:* Are lists of addresses of people in specific zip codes, or housing blocks, that you want to saturate with your acquisition efforts. These lists may or may not have the household resident's actual name embedded in the information you receive from the list company. The cheapest of all lists available, these lists are a real scatter shot. Since they saturate a specific geographic area, they will include addresses of people who have not demonstrated their responsiveness and may have little interest in your organization. It's a little like selling Girl Scout Cookies. Your mail carrier moves from house to house delivering your donor acquisition appeal, and you hope for the best.

4. *Co-op lists:* Are lists that are highly effective and include almost every household name in the United States. It does require your organization to join the co-op by submitting donor information so it may

require a review and/or modification of your current privacy policy to participate.

There, that's enough detailed talk about donor acquisition terms. I'm growing weary just writing these terms and definitions, so I imagine you might be tired of reading them as well.

Now let's go back to the beautiful shores of Vancouver Island for a moment. High-performing donor acquisition will require that we learn the terms of navigation and how to execute all the moves we'll need in order to avoid ending up submerged in the Graveyard of the Pacific!

I would be greatly amiss if I didn't tell you that the rules of donor acquisition dictate that you continuously acquire new donors. That's right; you never have enough new donors. Even if your goals aren't calling for rapid growth, you still have a problem. Every ship leaks! Your current numbers of existing donors are constantly dwindling. Not good news, I know. This ongoing process of dwindling is called donor attrition. It's a little bit like intestinal gas. Everybody has it, and nobody wants to admit it. The rules dictate, however, that every donor file dwindles, whether we want to acknowledge it to ourselves or not.

Many organizations decide to "take a year off" from donor acquisition, usually to manage the "expense side of the ledger." This is reminiscent of the ancient mariners' maps which read, "Beyond here there be sea monsters." It's a very dangerous place to go. By not spending the money to acquire new donors today, we are sailing dangerously.

Investing in our organization today will yield thousands, if not millions, of dollars within the next 5-6 years. As we develop our craft of responsible fundraising, we come to realize that acquiring new donors every year is not optional.

If money is extremely tight this year, you would do better to determine how many donors gave last year but not this year. This will give you a benchmark to, at the very least, replace those who stopped giving and keep your donor file stable for this year. Yes, it will still require an expenditure this fiscal year, but the cost will be less, and it will be saving you hundreds of thousands if not millions, of dollars in the next few years.

Just to give you an example of the value of future donations, a medium-sized rescue mission we serve has a net long-term donor value (LTDV) of $232.00. If they were to only acquire 1,000 new donors in a given year, it would net them $232,000 over six years. If they were to acquire

10,000 donors, the six-year net benefit would be $2,320,000!

This is why acquiring new donors is a continuous process and NEVER optional.

RULE #24

"What you think of people will determine how you treat them." Thoughts on Being a Major Donor

One of the things I'd really encourage you to do is to consider yourself a major donor. In fact, you probably are, because "major donor" means many things to many people and organizations. For some, a major donor is a person who gives $500 per year, for others it may require a gift of $5,000 or even $50,000. Think of it, if you give an organization $50 or $100 per month, you're giving them $600-$1,200 a year. For them you may be among their largest contributors.

Here's a true story about a couple who gave significant gifts and received very different responses: A few years ago, Mr. and Mrs. Jones entered a time when they were able to begin giving what most nonprofits would consider major gifts. And it has been really interesting to them to see how causes have responded to their gift giving:

Nonprofit Leader A, when informed of the Joneses' pending gift, instead of saying an appropriate "thank you" immediately asked, "Does this go against any existing pledge you've made to us?" In other words, "Should I be excited about this, or have I already counted it in my financial year?" How do you think this response made the Joneses feel?

A second Nonprofit, B, was given the Joneses' largest gift ever up to that point in time, and it was quite a sacrifice for them to give it that year. They were really excited that they did this. Mr. and Mrs. Jones received just a short, impersonal, handwritten phrase on a receipt letter... and that was it, for the entire year. No other involvement in their organization was offered...or given. No invitation to their annual banquet or major donor reception was forthcoming, and no other forms of thank you, other than the initial receipt letter, were given.

The next year, the Joneses decided to announce to Nonprofit C that their annual phone call requesting $150.00 was nice, but they were quite certain they must have greater needs and that they could likely receive additional support if they just asked. Mr. Jones gave them his business card during a local event and waited to see what happened. Wow! They listened!

Within days the Joneses received a phone call from the VP of advancement asking if they could have lunch when he was in town. During lunch he spoke about the organization and some of the exciting things they were doing (including a large capital campaign), but not once did he reference or ask the Joneses for a gift. He asked about their family and their business. He listened to who they were as well as what they did rather than what the Joneses could do for him and the nonprofit he served.

During lunch he told them about a special annual event held by the organization and asked the couple to consider attending. They said they would likely attend. Then Mr. Jones told him that they planned on making what the Joneses perceived would be a nice gift but nothing like what they knew other donors were giving. The generous couple even told him the expected amount and when they would likely give it. He smiled, said, "Thank you," and then promptly changed the subject back to happenings at his organization. Being an experienced philanthropist, Mr. Jones asked the vice president how best to designate their upcoming gift. The vice president thought for a moment and then indicated a specific ongoing fund but not the capital campaign that he had just mentioned.

True to his word, the VP of advancement for Nonprofit C sent a nice follow-up letter indicating that the Joneses should be receiving an invitation to their special annual event. The invitation came about three weeks later, and they accepted.

The special annual event lasted three days, and the couple loved it. Everything was well organized, on time and of the excellent quality one would expect from this group. During this time, Mr. Jones presented the VP of advancement with their gift in a closed envelope. He smiled, said, "Thank you," and mentioned his appreciation later during the event. Then it got quiet...

Several months went by and the Joneses heard nothing from Nonprofit C. Mrs. Jones felt that maybe they had expected a larger gift than she and her husband had given and so maybe the organization wasn't as interested in them anymore. After all, the organization's upcoming capital campaign was so huge, and the Joneses knew they couldn't make a dent in it.

One day Mr. Jones received an introductory call from the new regional representative of Nonprofit C. She informed him of their intent to hold a series of capital campaign meetings around the country and asked him if he would consider not only attending a regional planning committee meeting but also chairing it. It made Mr. Jones feel wanted and important, but he knew his schedule wouldn't allow. He called back later and left a phone message indicating that he and his wife would indeed attend the November regional event and support the campaign financially, but neither he nor his wife could be on or chair the regional committee.

Several months later Mr. Jones received a formal invitation to the regional event followed up by a phone call. During the call, Nonprofit C's representative informed him that the organization would love to go into the event with some funds already pledged from their area, had he and Mrs. Jones discussed what they thought they could do? He told her that they had indeed decided to make a gift and told her the amount.

Here's where the representative earned her money... she asked two very valuable questions:

1. Will this be over and above your annual fund giving?
2. Can we expect that you will be willing to give this same capital campaign gift amount each year for

the next three years (the duration of the campaign)?

Mr. Jones answered "yes" to both questions. She was delighted and said so. Her enthusiasm was very encouraging and unexpected. The couple had assumed wrongly that their gift would not be that big of a deal, given the large contributions by some of the organization's other donors. Then Mr. Jones did something that surprised even him. He called his wife, and they both agreed to round up their total pledge to six figures over 3 years (over and above their recent annual giving amount).

Mr. Jones knew when he called Nonprofit C's representative back and connected with her voice mail, she would be worried that he and his wife had changed their minds. As expected, she called right back with no small amount of worry in her voice.

But he told her he was calling to increase their pledge. Again, a huge demonstration of excitement! She told Mr. Jones, with his permission, she would be sharing this information with the president of the nonprofit. Of course he agreed. She also asked if she could share the dollar amount of the Joneses' gift (along with the giving of others) with the attendees of the regional event (of course the Joneses' names would not be divulged). This would be done to encourage others to give or pledge that evening.

The night of the event was a very special time for the Jones couple. They felt excitement about hearing the president speak and seeing their representative, as well as the VP of advancement.

They also wanted to hear more about how the capital campaign was progressing. When the Joneses arrived, they were warmly welcomed by several members of the development staff, as well as the president and his wife. The couple felt special indeed!

As the Joneses looked around the room that night, they remembered praying that others would feel led to give generously to the capital campaign. They both felt as though they were on the team, true partners with this organization.

Mr. and Mrs. Jones were to later learn that their pledge had been a great encouragement to the development team and the president. The nonprofit had held another event earlier in the week, in the same region, and it had been much less fruitful. The generous couple felt, "They indeed needed us!"

Now, let me say Nonprofit C did not do everything right. There were several long stretches where communication could have cleared up the Joneses' concerns or questions. The transition from the V.P. for advancement to the new regional representative could have been handled with more aplomb.

But the Joneses' belief in the mission of the organization, coupled with their obvious and genuine excitement at the Joneses' financial commitment by Nonprofit C made the couple want to be even more involved.

All of this brings me to how we look at our donors. Do we see them for the treasured creatures of God they are, or do we see them only as a means to our end? Are we here to serve them or to use them? Are we caring deeply about them, or are we praying they'll make a swift journey to paradise so we can finally hear the reading of their wills?

Of course, we're here to help them make wise investments of the money they entrust to us. We all know this. We wouldn't have embarked on the great voyage of philanthropic encouragement if we didn't deeply care about people.

But I think it's worth pausing for a moment and looking closely at how we are communicating with our donors. Are we being intentional in our communication? By this I mean, are we thinking about the donor first, or are we giving into the many pressures of development and just trying to achieve our income forecast?

It might be good for us to consider the fact that we really don't have any donors. They don't really belong to us. They could just as easily give their gifts to some other great cause, but they've decided to support our organization. I've come to see that donors themselves are a gift from God! So just how do we become more intentional in our communication with those who support our cause?

A few months before I founded Douglas Shaw & Associates, in October of 1994, I began to embrace the idea of communicating *with* donors instead of talking *at* them. One of my dearest clients noticed it first. One day she asked me, "Doug, have you seen this great article on fundraising letter writing by Con Squires?" I took a look. A light went on that is still lit today! Fabled direct mail copywriter Conrad Squires had written a wonderful letter demonstrating the value of writing to the donor rather than about the nonprofit.

The more I pondered this insight, the more excited I became. Of course, people would like to be included or featured in communication sent to them; after all, we're in this together! So, I began urging my employer to become more "donor-focused" in the copy our agency was writing. He wasn't particularly interested in my input to the creative process, so I dropped it for the time being. I decided to savor the idea until I could start my own company.

As it turned out, this was all for the best. It gave me time to think through my own personal philosophy and theology of fundraising and communication. And the more I thought about it, it made even more sense. Here's what I've discovered: Most nonprofits are what I would call Institutionally-Focused in their communication and fundraising. Here's an example:

Let's say you go out to dinner with a friend. All evening long, your friend just talks about herself. You hardly get a word in edgewise. As the evening wears on you begin sneaking peeks at your watch under the guise of making sure your nail polish isn't chipped. You make a note to self: "Don't do this again anytime soon!"

I've come to realize that this is what happens when we communicate with donors without taking them into consideration. Let me elaborate. Over the years I've seen nonprofits do their best to inform the donors to their organization that they are indeed worthy of the gifts being sent to them. Many times, this involves statements like, "Last month we helped our community by providing 1,000 meals to senior citizens." This is great. It shows the donor that their gift really made a difference in the lives of deserving people.

Now let's try this same statement, only this time, let's shift the focus to the donor. I call it being Donor-Focused: "Last month, because of your generosity, 1,000 meals were provided to the senior citizens of our community. Thank you so much for caring!" Subtle, isn't it? It's only a few degrees of difference. The first statement is Institutionally-Focused. It conveys similar information, but it doesn't credit the donor with being a part of the solution. The second statement is Donor-Focused. This approach or philosophy quietly moves your organization out of the way, but not out of the picture. It places the emphasis where it needs to be; i.e., on the people who give, pray or volunteer!

This intentional philosophy of fundraising and communication requires practice to consistently employ. If you find yourself being the primary writer for your organization, or overseeing the writing, there's a helpful ritual you may want to employ. First, write the way you normally do. Then, sit back, take a deep breath and *write the donor into it.* The less "we" language you use the better. "You," "your" and phrases like, "Thanks to you" are signs that you're taking the donor into account.

I've had significant resistance to this approach over the years. I think the most gracious of the criticisms has been, "It's sappy!" Let them call it what they will; I'm above it. It doesn't hurt my feelings...much. What really matters is, does it work? I have consistently found that it does. You may want to test it on your next donor appeal. You can do this by writing your appeal the way you normally do, and then, using only this one variable, *write the donor into the appeal.* I think you'll be pleased with the results.

We take this philosophy so seriously here at Douglas Shaw & Associates that we've trademarked the phrase: Donor- Focused Strategic Marketing™. It's our experience that using this philosophy coupled with The 5 Commandments of Offer Development (Rule #8) will increase most nonprofits' income, regardless of the communication channel used.

RULE #25

"Just because a person has a lot of money, doesn't mean they'll give it to you."

This can seem, at first glance, to be a rather unfair rule. You are, after all, working for one of the most compelling charities in the world. But fundraising is much more than just finding wealthy people and asking them to give great globs of money. There is so much more to giving than just having the capacity to give. Let me tell you about Sam the Ice Cream Man...

Sam's business has done better than he ever expected. In fact, he just sold his company to one of the big multinational food corporations for $40 million. You may have read about it in the business pages of your local newspaper or seen it online. A lightbulb goes off in your head! "This guy could fund our entire organization for the next 10 years! But how do I get him to part with his money?"

Before you consider walking into your president's office and announcing your new long-term funding plan, give yourself a few minutes or even a full hour to review what you know about Sam the Ice Cream Man. Here are a few questions that might be of help:

1. Does Sam know your organization exists?
2. Has Sam ever given to your cause?
3. Has Sam ever given a financial gift to anyone that you know of?

Let's suppose Sam has heard of your organization; in fact he's donated ice cream to the kids you serve, and he's done it every month for the past six years. You've also heard that he supplies several other local organizations with ice cream.

One time you even had all your kids build this giant fudgesicle with their signed names and glued their handwritten notes of appreciation all over it. You delivered it one afternoon with two of the cutest kids in your program. Sam was delighted and agreed to have his picture taken with the kids and the fudgesicle, which you promptly used in your newsletter. Now the thought comes to you, "Certainly he'll consider breaking off some of that vast fortune of his to help our kids!"

I'd like to add a word of caution here. If you've read about the sale of Sam's company so has every other charitable institution in town. But even more important is that you continue asking questions:

1. Has Sam ever given us a cash gift? If so, what was the amount?
2. Have you ever heard of Sam giving cash gifts to any other organization?
3. Who is Sam? What does he believe? What are his values?
4. Have you or anyone connected with your organization ever spent quality time with Sam, giving him a solid understanding of who you serve and the scope of your work with kids?
5. Do you care about Sam as a person? Does he know it?
6. Does Sam love what you do in the community? In the country? In the world? How has he expressed it?

7. What have you done to keep Sam carefully and personally informed about how his gifts are helping children?

If, like me, you're getting a little uncomfortable with this line of questioning, there's probably a good reason. It may be that Sam the Ice Cream Man does not really feel connected to your cause in a deeply meaningful way. He may simply be a kind and generous gift-in-kind donor to many organizations.

After spending an hour or so asking these types of questions, you may want to adjust the announcement you were about to make to your president. It may be that you use this knowledge of Sam and your relationship, or perhaps lack of relationship, to resolve to spend more time loving and caring for your donors, in ways that are meaningful to them.

Two weeks have gone by and you read, again in your local paper, that Sam has just made a $10 million gift to the Children's Memorial Hospital! The article explains that Sam's grandson, "little Sam," was treated there for leukemia. While "little Sam" didn't survive, Sam the Ice Cream Man has established a "little Sam" research endowment so other children can live. Once you choke back your tears of joy at seeing the kindness of Sam's heart, along with a twinge of disappointment and jealousy, you may want to use this experience to do something generous. A note of congratulations to the president of Children's Memorial Hospital might be a great place to begin. You may even want to have your own president write a note to Sam, telling him that you admire him for what he has done. This is also an opportunity to build a closer relationship, so that, in the future, you can also ask Sam to become more familiar with your cause, and when the time is right, ask him for a sizable gift!

If you are just beginning to work with donors or prospects that have significant capacities to give, you may find The Institute for Charitable Giving helpful in launching or refreshing your major gifts program. They offer a two-day intensive course called Seize the Opportunity™. They do a terrific job of helping train people who are involved or want to be involved in major gift fundraising.

RULE #26

"The best direct response donors are women 55 and older."

This is a long-standing rule in direct response. It was true 30 years ago when I entered the marketplace, and it remains true today. But given the way the world is changing its channels of communication, this rule may not hold true tomorrow. (See Rule #33.)

Direct response includes direct mail, but it includes other fundraising channels as well. It can also mean: radio, direct response television (DRTV), websites, e-mail, social media and any other form of communication where an "offer" is presented with the expectation of a gift.

I remember asking, "Why are 55-year-old and older women the best respondents?" Here's what my mentors have taught me...because they are the most responsive, according to any verifiable testing conducted throughout the marketplace. We may not like this rule because it feels limiting and perhaps even sexist. But the plain truth is, 55-year-old and older women give at a much higher rate than say, 45-year-old men and women.

Thirty-four years ago, I was 30. I didn't like the idea of marketing to people who were my mother's age. I wanted to create fundraising appeals that I could personally relate to.

I remember thinking back then, "This is old school thinking. My generation is different." So, I rolled the dice against conventional wisdom and bloodied my nose several times.

After a while I got so tired of stuffing Kleenex in my face that I began to read and listen more closely to those who were having success with marketing to women aged 55 and over.

I learned that more women check the mailbox than men. More women are emotionally moved by people in need than men. I didn't like this fact, but all I had to do was glance at the Kleenex box and it would bring me running back to reality.

Okay, so I gave in grudgingly, but I did eventually give in. But why do women have to be 55 or older? Again, the sages available to me explained patiently, by age 55 many people's mortgages are paid off, the kids are grown and out of college. Also, not only are women more apt to respond to the heart messages of fundraising, but they get the mail from the mailbox, and they decide what to keep and what to toss. They also have more money than someone a decade younger than they are because they've already bought the big things of life like furniture, carpets, jewelry, clothes, etc. They have more disposable income.

Again, when I was younger, another related question came to my mind. The organization I was working for had an aging donor base. I remember meetings where people were saying, "Our donors are so old that they're all going to die pretty soon. We've got to get to the younger donor!" This cry was heard all across the land. Seminars sprang up about how Baby Boomers were not going to give like their Builder parents. Discussions of how to reach Gen Xers were always good for a crowd too.

But here I am, bald, not-so-svelte, I traded in my luxury sedan for a pickup truck, and my kids are grown.

The organizations who were, in the early 1980s, writing eulogies for their donors are still here, and many have grown substantially. Who are supporting these great causes? Largely women, aged 55 and older.

Not long ago, one of our very talented vice presidents came into my office with the joyful news that he had just received a call from one of our clients. A 90-year-old woman had just sent a check for $400,000! He rejoiced and then said, "This'll really screw up our average gift on this appeal!" I responded with a smile, "What a tough problem to have!"

Now a few words about younger donors from Eric Streiff, a business colleague:

"I believe there are many young people who want to make a difference, and nonprofits need to tap into this paradigm shift over the next few years. The discretionary income of the under-30 crowd is significant, and it wouldn't be a stretch for them to give up four Starbucks lattes every month and give the $20 saved to charity. I think the younger crowd gets this concept and will make the sacrifice to help someone. So, in this case, the rule of thumb is changing, and perhaps in our lifetime we will begin to see more and more younger people supporting charities."

I share Eric's hope and confidence in the young people of our world. But I'm still going to employ the Kleenex knowledge as well as Ronald Reagan's principle that he so often stated, "Trust but verify!" We don't have to guess about the giving patterns of younger people, because we can always test!

In 2008 an Intergenerational Transmission of Generosity study was released by the Center on Philanthropy Panel (COPPS). This is a very reputable source. The study confirmed, once again, what my experience and early mentors had been saying all along: people's values change with age, especially if giving is modeled by their parents.

Baby Boomers are indeed giving, much like their parents. My guess is Gen Xers and Millennials will do the same when they approach this wonderful age of financial and material fulfillment. The nice thing about our target audience is, much like Doritos, God is making more of them!

According to U.S. Census data women 55 and older increased in their percentage of the overall U.S. population from 2000 (23%) to 2010 (26%). This is good news for fundraisers. Even more good news is coming, in that the same census study indicates in the decade following the 2010 census, 55 and older females will make up even more of the U.S. population. There is indeed hope!

RULE #27

"Premiums can help increase giving and premiums can suppress giving."

It's not my intention to try and be confusing here. It's the rule itself that's confusing. You may have heard National Public Radio fundraising drives on your local public radio station. You know, it's that annoying 2-3 days where you have to listen to some other station or whistle to yourself in the car. I'm sure you've also heard, "And, if you give a gift of $30 or more today, you'll receive a coffee mug featuring our program 'Morning Edition' as our way of saying thank you!" It must work for them, since they've been doing it for years. It also squares with my own experience in funding broadcast organizations.

Direct response is an excellent venue for the use of premiums. This can include any direct response mechanism, e.g., direct mail, radio, direct response television (DRTV), websites, email blasts, social media ads and mobile giving.

If you'll permit me, I'd like to examine the nature of meaningful premiums for organizations where they are, indeed, used effectively. I once again interviewed Wiley Stinnett.

(By the way, these same principles also apply to nonreligious organizations.) Here are some of the salient points that came from this discussion. A meaningful premium has a number of elements to it regardless of the channel used to promote it:

1. It has to meet a spiritual need of the individual to whom it's being offered.

2. It must fit the "calling" of the ministry; e.g., if a ministry is a bible teaching ministry and the selected premium is about evangelism, it's not a fit. Another example of a mismatched premium would be to offer a book about "How to Raise Your Child" to the donors of a ministry who are known to be elderly. Since the ministry is perceived to be a ministry to the elderly, your organization would not be perceived to need competency in the area of child-rearing.

3. In broadcast media, premiums can be used in many
different ways. By offering an appropriate premium, a ministry can acquire names and donors, re-
activate lapsed donors and keep its active donors
engaged. In this case, an appropriate premium has
to meet the criteria in numbers 1 and 2 above, plus
it has to have a perceived value. It also has to meet
a perceived need on the individual listener or
viewer's part.

Whew! Did you get all of that? I'm not sure I did. Let
me try to translate or "channel" Wiley just for a moment: People will respond to premiums they find
meaningful, but it may well meet even deeper needs
than they think they have. If it meets a deeper need,
they will be even more grateful that you offered it
to them.

Many years ago, a beloved client, Dr. Erwin Lutzer,
Pastor Emeritus of Chicago's Moody Church, wrote
a very informative book, One Minute After You Die.
Not only is the title relevant to all readers, but it creates curiosity. Everybody's going to face death at
some point, so personal relevance is very high.

Many people chose to read this book to satisfy their curiosity about what was going to happen to them. But Pastor Lutzer began receiving letter after letter of how people's lives had been impacted by his book. Some people expressed appreciation for such a clear statement of the afterlife. Others wrote indicating the book had deepened their faith. The most rewarding responses, for Pastor Lutzer, were those who wrote to tell him that the book had encouraged them to embrace faith for the first time in their lives.

4. In effective direct mail, the reason a person gives is not to receive a premium. They may give to cover a financial shortfall, to help with an emergency or even to take full advantage of a once-in-a-lifetime opportunity for your cause. In this case, the premium is merely a "thank you for helping us." This approach wisely distances the size of the gift from the perceived value of the premium. They may well give a $500.00 gift and receive a $14.95 book as a "thank you." The difference in giving to an organization's mission vs. giving to receive a book is subtle but significant.

There's something you may want to watch out for here. What you want to achieve with a premium is to provide a premium that is low-cost to the organization but has a high perceived value. There's a trap that many people fall into here; they offer a high-cost premium with high perceived value and end up losing money in the process. For example, an organization might have thousands of books in their warehouse and offer them on-air or through some other channel for a gift of any amount and lose money in the process. The big question here is, "Why are the books sitting in your warehouse?" The likely answer is, "They didn't sell." This alone should be a warning signal to you. If a person wouldn't buy the book, why would they give more than the book is worth as a premium?

Organizations may well rationalize their actions because they've already incurred the cost of having the product in existing inventory. But corporate memory tends to be short. Later, when reviewing the value of using premiums, they may decide that the cost/income ratio isn't worth it. But they've forgotten that their information is skewed because they factored in expensive warehouse books.

When selecting premiums, it's vital that we look at the cost of the premium, its size, the packaging, shipping costs and the postage vs. the size of the average gift we expect to receive. By the way, most premiums should not cost much over $10.00 including shipping and postage. If we decide to "bend the rule" because we have something so special that we choose to offer it to the donor anyway, we need to do it with our eyes wide open. In other words, we need to document our assumptions so we don't forget that we bent the rules intentionally, and we would do well to review our results in light of our intended purpose, which in this case may be to get something of great value into our donor's hands and not necessarily to maximize income.

Now, here at Douglas Shaw & Associates, we use premiums for several of the organizations we serve, but it requires fairly sophisticated knowledge of the rules and variables surrounding this whole premium thing. If you don't have this knowledge, you might want to get help from someone who has made mistakes and knows how to avoid them; for example, there are many organizations that do not and should not use premiums. In most cases, social services organizations like relief and development organizations, food banks, child sponsorship organizations and the like should generally not use premiums. Organizations that are helping to care for the basic needs that keep people alive will find premiums an obstacle to building relationships with their donors.

Why is this? It comes down to the 5 commandments of offer construction (see Rule #8).

There is a disconnect, in the donor's mind, between giving $20 to help feed, shelter or clothe a person and being offered a $8 premium for their generous gift. Why not spend the $8 you're paying for the premium to help save or change even more lives?

Even the extra postage you spent to send them a premium might be offensive. The bottom line is premiums are seldom, if ever, helpful to social services organizations; they can, however, be essential to many other kinds of causes like educational institutions, broadcasters and other organizations that are not involved in life-or-death issues. As I mentioned, great care should be used when considering the price and the donor's perceived value of the premium.

RULE #28

"A donor is better than a buyer except when she's both."

If your nonprofit sells curriculum, books, CDs, DVDs, MP3s or anything else that rhymes with E, you may want to read on.

This little gem of a rule has caused more than one shouting match between development and marketing departments within charities. The problem stems from the fact that products are very tangible, can be sold for a specific price and can be used to encourage to constituents. There's a very comforting sense to transactions of this type.

Products can educate, articulate and communicate the very essence of your mission. What can possibly be wrong with this? Nothing, if what we are looking for are buyers and not donors. So, you sell a very good product for $14.95, and it costs you only $5.95 to make, package and ship it to someone who's eagerly awaiting it. That's a net profit of $9.00 (yes, I used a calculator to derive this number)! The only problem with acquiring buyers is they have a purchasing relationship, not a giving relationship. Once the purchase is complete, they generally do not convert to donors. Usually only about 5-10% will ever cross the line to donor status after one year of ongoing monthly cultivation. This is about the same conversion rate that you will achieve by cultivating and converting non-donors into donors.

Let's look at another kind of product transaction. A person responds to an appeal made through the mailbox, online or over the air. Let's say they give an initial gift of $30.00, which is pretty average for most first gifts. This time you have done something radical here. You've decided to offer them this same product, costing you $5.95, for FREE, NADA, NOTHING, as your way of saying "thank you" for their gift (some marketing people have been seen becoming physically ill at this point).

Yes, your profit margin is higher, which according to my Texas Instruments calculator is $24.05. Now subtract from this the cost of making your appeal. Just for argument's sake, let's say your fundraising cost is $5.00 (much more than most direct mail packages). You net $19.05. But there's more! In this transaction you gain a donor, someone who has responded to the mission of your organization.

What you have just done is acquired a donor vs. a buyer! But here comes the best part of the rule: "except when she's a donor and a buyer." A donor will give because they believe in your cause, thereby gaining a longer, more financially viable relationship. But it gets even better.

Once a donor has given at least two gifts, you can sell them products all day long and it will only enhance their relationship with your organization. Many people don't understand the significance of this rule. The counter-intuitive nature of it is just too much for some people to grasp. That's why all the fistfights break out between marketing and fundraising! The person in the marketing department is tasked with selling products; this is logical, respectable and often necessary. But fundraising, as we've often said, is counter intuitive. Giving away a product with high perceived value for a gift of any amount will result in an average donation of $20-$30.

Again the venerable Wiley Stinnett, our SVP for Strategic Insights:

"There's a phenomenon that I've observed. If a product is offered for sale through a catalog or product insert to 2,000,000 buyers, an organization might sell 500 to 1,000 units. If the very same product is offered as an open-ended offer (upon request, whether a gift is given or not) or as a 'Thank you' for a gift of any amount, the end result is a response rate of 12-15%, or in this case 240,000-300,000 units, most of which result in donations at the same time!"

So, a donor is better than a buyer, unless she is both a donor and a buyer.

If you're in marketing and you're still reading, you've tolerated more marketing heresy than most. You should be proud of yourself! Most marketing folks would have tossed this book in the trash by now. If you're a fundraiser and you've found this book in the trash can in your marketing department, slip it under your sweater, just smile innocently and walk quietly out of the room.

The important lesson in this rule is that when a donor is engaged as a donor first and then becomes a buyer, a stronger relational and financial link is formed. That's why it's better to acquire donors first and then, after two gifts, sell products to them.

RULE #29

"Multi-channel donors make the best donors."

At the time of writing, the hot phrase in fundraising is "Multi-channel Marketing." Of course, by tomorrow it will be something else. But for now, while it's still blazing, let's wade into the fray!

The simple truth is that the more channels a donor uses to give to your organization, the better donor they become. I'll discuss the reason for this in just a moment.

Several years ago, my colleague Michael and I went to the annual Blackbaud® Conference (a very large software provider to nonprofits) in Charleston, South Carolina. We were privileged to deliver yet another seminar for their software users. Our presentation was part of the "Online Track." Now, we weren't totally certain we belonged in the "online track" because so much of what we were presenting was broader than giving from online sources. You see, we're so interested in what actually generates donations that we struggle with separating channels into tracks. Here's what Michael told the attendees at the Blackbaud® Conference:

"About 10% of the donations raised for the clients we serve comes from online sources; 90% comes from offline." Since the initial writing of this book these figures have changed to 30% online and 70% offline. Now this isn't exactly what you'd expect to hear at a software conference. But it's true! It helps make this more plausible to realize this includes ALL offline giving sources including major gifts, estates, grants, special events and all the direct response channels too.

To illustrate his point, Michael presented the following chart from a nonprofit we serve:

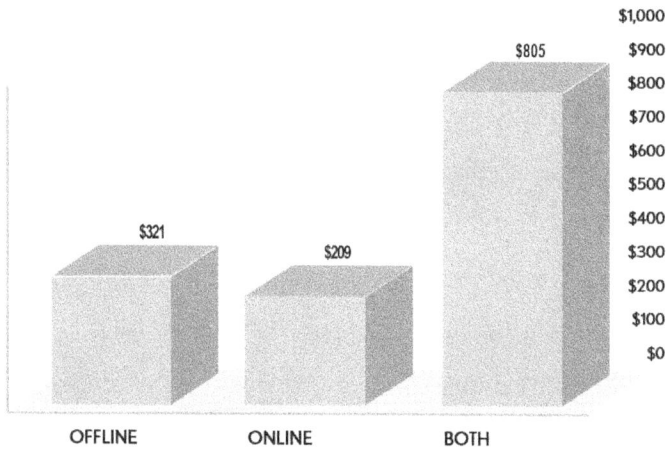

ACTUAL NONPROFIT'S AVERAGE VALUE BY CHANNEL - 2024

Now the real point of this rule is the advantages you will gain by using multiple channels to communicate the same offer and message to your donors. As the graph indicates, donors who begin to use more than one channel, especially an online channel and an offline channel, become far more engaged with your cause and provide significantly more income.

How do you engage donors in multi-channel giving? That's what I'd be asking if I was reading this for the first time.

It's not terribly difficult to accomplish if you remember to integrate all that you do in your fundraising program. Here's an example:

Let's say you are planning to raise money for housing for those assisting bible translators. These would be the indigenous folks who are helping the translators better understand the language and culture of the people for whom the new translation is directed.

Your strategy will need to come first; using the 5 Commandments of Rule #8, determine the 5 Critical Components of an Effective Offer. As part of your strategy, you'll need to determine the optimal channels for communicating this giving opportunity to your donors. Direct mail is still one of the foundational channels for any nonprofit's fundraising (or should be). In your creative process for your appeal, you can, on your reply slip, by using a QR code, direct your donors to your website, micro-site or a special landing page that gives more details about the need for housing. Here you can use more photos/video, etc. If the donor chooses to give their gift online, fantastic! If you're like most charities, you don't really care which channel a donor chooses for their gift, as long as they give. This process will increase the number of direct mail donors who are also giving online, thus becoming donors through both offline and online channels.

Now take this same approach with all of your offline channels and you will see an influx in your online giving.

Please don't misunderstand my point here. You are not trying to do away with direct mail as a fundraising channel; you are simply trying to expand your donor engagement into additional channels, thereby increasing their engagement, which will, in turn, increase the amount they contribute. This is worth pursuing because, as this rule states: Multi-channel donors make the best donors.

RULE #30

"Never use more than one offer in a request for funds."

So you're sitting in your conference room, and all the usual players are assembled. It's time to plan the strategy for one of your biggest direct mail appeals of the year. The CEO has joined you because of the amount of money expected from this effort and, besides, she has a few ideas she'd like to throw out on the table.

As the director of development, you have prepared a Creative Strategy Brief (CSB). This is a document that outlines all the salient facts, messaging, segmentation and offer to be used.

As the one who has convened this meeting, you begin walking the group through the CSB. But now the CEO decides it's time to broach the new ideas she's been pondering: "I've been doing some thinking about this appeal. I know we usually only talk about one thing in every appeal, but this time, I'd like for us to consider presenting two critical initiatives for our donors to consider. It's absolutely essential that we generate funding for both of these. In fact, if we fund just the new broadcast equipment, it won't do us any good if we don't hire the new programmers we need to operate it. So, in my way of thinking, we can let the donors choose which initiative they'd like to fund, the equipment or the people, or hopefully both. Your thoughts?" she says looking around the table. The operations manager for radio chimes in, "I love it!" But everyone else sits there kind of quiet. Most are looking at the top of the conference table. You shift uncomfortably in your chair, looking again at the CSB document you've so carefully crafted, you take a deep breath and raise your eyes to meet the gaze of the CFO, who's sitting just opposite of you. The CEO is now looking directly at you, from her seat at the end of the table. In fact, everybody in the room is looking at you.

What do you say?

We've all been there at one time or another. And there's nothing fun about it. The pressure you feel to agree with the CEO is exceeded only by your knowledge of the Rules of Fundraising. You know that the easy way out, to agree with the CEO, will only be easy for the next 10 minutes. Once the meeting's adjourned the burden of producing significant income still falls to you.

Looking over at the CFO, you begin to speak, rather softly at first. "Well, we could use two options for donors, but there is a conflict that I'm feeling about it." The CFO is looking at you expectantly. He's hoping you'll dissuade the CEO so he won't have to do it. You resume, a little more confidence in your voice and word choices now, "My conflict comes from my experience. Every time we've presented more than one offer in a letter to donors, we've missed our target income." The CFO has been waiting for this opening, and he jumps on it. "That's right, Susan," he says to the CEO, "We've tried multiple options in appeal letters twice in the last two years, and both times we didn't make budget."

All eyes rise from the table and look first to the CFO and then slowly pan toward the end of the conference table.

Susan looks up at the ceiling, leans back in her chair and lets out her breath...

Ending A: "Alright, you're the ones with the experience. I yield. But we are going to need to fund both initiatives. So let me know what you come up with."

Ending B: "I know our donors, and I think you're underestimating them. They're going to want us to have what we need. Let's let them vote on what's a priority by offering them both. I'm convinced it's going to work."

Now I know when you find yourself in this situation, you're sitting there praying for Ending A. But the real ending will depend upon your knowledge of the Rules of Fundraising, how well you have taught your leadership team what they are and the personal and professional trust that you've built with them, especially the CEO.

Those who know their craft know that more than one offer will sidetrack the donor's attention and result in lower response. This is true for direct mail but also any other channel available to you.

As a CEO, you are responsible for advancing the mission of your organization, but you are also responsible for the highest levels of return on the investments you make. I encourage you to trust your development team; if they have demonstrated that they know what they're doing (e.g., through the use of the Rules of Fundraising) you would be leading well by responding with Ending A.

Board members also need to know enough about the Rules of Fundraising to trust your CEO and development team. You don't need to know all about the rules, but you need to know that they exist and must be followed. Your role here is to ensure that your organization's fundraising ratios are in line with expectations that will qualify your charity to receive foundation grants, receive favorable ratings by groups like Charity Navigator and have the full confidence of your donors and potential donors.

RULE #31

"Effective fundraising strategies and approaches vary by country and culture."

Our company has had the distinct honor and privilege of serving in Canada. To my delight, our efforts there have exceeded most expectations.

I travel to Canada frequently, and I thoroughly enjoy my time there. I do okay with kilometers instead of miles, but I still get pretty confused over Celsius vs. Fahrenheit. My hotel room is usually too hot or too cold for the first few hours until I figure it out. The currency is another difference. We don't have toonies (a two-dollar coin) or loonies (a one-dollar coin featuring a loon) here in the U.S.; some Canadians have commented to me their frustration that all American paper currency looks the same. But the differences in culture extend far beyond the metric and monetary systems of our two nations.

Eric Streiff, a business colleague, had the experience of being an American serving as the executive director of a Canadian nonprofit. His insight into the U.S. and Canadian cultural distinctive is worth noting: "Americans tolerate hard-nosed tactics while Canadians abhor them." I find this to be my own experience as well, and it extends far beyond fundraising. There is a civility in Canadian culture that I have known for many years, that doesn't easily come through here in the States. There is also a precision and tone to Canadian writing and conversation that is often found missing in the everyday communications of Americans. We have so much in common, yet the word choices, tone and cultural context are quite distinctly Canadian. Even the spelling of English words can be different. Check it out on your computer. There is a language selection for Canadian English! Believe me, Canadians notice this difference.

The late, great Canadian historian Pierre Berton's writings are filled with nuances and cultural influences that help the reader to understand the parallel tracks our two countries have taken. For example, Berton speaks of the differences between the Europeans migrating across

Canada and those who participated in the westward movement in the United States.

There were no local sheriffs in Canadian towns, but rather the presence of a national force of Royal Canadian Mounted Police; we may best know them as "Mounties." In the States, an outlaw could shoot the sheriff and go on about his business, but not in Canada. There was an endless line of Mounties, who were known to "Always get their man." In Berton's thinking, this made Canada a more orderly country.

Berton notes another significant difference between Canada and the United States. While both nations have deep roots in Western Europe, the Americans had a revolution against the British Empire while the Canadians had a peaceful transfer of power. These differences shaped our countries in significant ways that remain today.

In fundraising, as in culture, there are distinctive differences between American and Canadian giving practices. First of all, churchgoers make up a much smaller portion of the population in Canada than they do in the U.S., and those who do attend, appear to be more denominationally oriented. Their culture tends to be more government-dependent for meeting social needs. Also, Canadians have more quickly adapted to monthly giving than Americans. Online giving accounts for more of the charitable giving in Canada than it does here in the U.S. Americans currently give 70% of their charitable gifts offline, still choosing to write checks, and, as of the time of writing, 30% or less online. But the rules are certainly in flux on this issue as we continue to adapt to the rapidly changing technology available to us.

Marketing and advertising greats Al Reis and Jack Trout in their fascinating book, Positioning: The Battle for the Mind, make the point that the United States has twice the amount of advertising as Canada. This can be a boon for Canadian fundraisers. There is less need to shout in order to be heard.

I've been told by a German media mogul that, in Germany, most charitable giving occurs at the post office or online. A person, entering the post office, can choose from a wall of envelopes from officially recognized charities and place their donation into the envelope and mail it directly to their charity of choice. Another distinctive in Germany is that the use of checks, for giving, has virtually become extinct. As mentioned, such is not the case here in the U.S., but with the use of Paypal, Apple Pay, Venmo and others, checks are less and less part of our lives.

A few years ago I had the privilege of being invited to speak at the Christian Media Association conference in Surfer's Paradise, a beautiful east coast beach city just to the south of Brisbane, Australia. There I found radio and television media ministries soaking up the Rules of Fundraising as fast as I could deliver them.

Australian and New Zealand broadcast programming is quite different from that of the U.S. There, the government plays a more active role in the licensing and content of broadcasters' activities. But there is more to it than this.

Christian broadcasting in New Zealand and Australia has far fewer political overtones, and there are a growing number of "mixed" stations, i.e., stations that include both religious and nonreligious content.

My point here is each culture has its own take on the rules of communication and fundraising; an example being marketing to Latinos, which is an explosive opportunity for fundraisers who know the cultures, not only here in the U.S. and in Latin American countries, but wherever there are high concentrations of Latinos. This often requires organizations to partner with Latino marketing firms in order to get it right.

My first experience with marketing within the Latino culture came in 1988 while serving as a consultant to

World Vision, U.S. This required a partnership with an agency in Santa Monica, California. They served as much more than translators by making certain our messaging was culturally appropriate. This careful consideration of cultural differences proved highly successful for World Vision.

The dangers of ignoring cultural differences can perhaps best be demonstrated by the old story of the marketing efforts of the now defunct Braniff Airlines. They meant to encourage business by blanketing their routes in Latin America with, "When you fly Braniff, you fly in leather!" referring to the leather seats being featured in all of their aircraft. As the story goes, the campaign rolled out in Spanish with some errors in cultural translation that resulted in a slogan which said, "Fly Braniff and fly naked!" This wasn't a niche marketing effort to nudists; it was a significant lack of understanding of language and culture. Our cross-cultural effectiveness is dependent upon our willingness to become a student of our target markets. Asking questions still outweighs making assumptions, especially in this world economy. Respect for culturally distinctive communication is something we Americans can consider a growth opportunity.

RULE #32

"Sometimes the rules change."

As much as I desire stability in my life, there are times when predictability and constancy still evade me. When September 11, 2001, came around, it stood the world on its head. The good people of New York City; Arlington, Virginia; and Shanksville, Pennsylvania, will never hear the sound of a jet flying overhead in the same way ever again. Even those of us who didn't live in one of the areas under direct attack have been permanently changed by the events of that fateful morning and the years of warfare that have followed.

The nation was in both shock and mourning. We had not only lost family members, friends and loved ones, but we had lost our long-held belief that we were impenetrable to the outside forces of destruction; our security had been wrested away from us.

The stock market plummeted, by presidential mandate the airlines were grounded; many feeder industries to these critical pillars in our economic system were highly affected as well. For post-World War II generations it was clearly our "Pearl Harbor."

I used to live in one of the western suburbs of Chicago that serves as a flight path for O'Hare International Airport, so I remember clearly, on September 12th, how quiet the skies were. It was an eerie, unwelcome silence.

I also remember how I tore myself away from the television and walked to the grocery store with my son, Graham, who was 14 at the time. We chose to walk the mile and a half each way so that we could just be together and see people, just ordinary people trying to go about their daily lives. It was a feeling of solidarity I will never forget.

Complete strangers nodded to each other and a bonding was occurring in our community and all over the country as messages of shock and condolences poured in from people and their governments all over the world. When I got home, I pounded a huge spike into the frame of one of my front windows and hung up my American flag!

As fundraisers, we all felt the reverberations throughout our industry too. Billions of dollars in private contributions flowed to the areas of attack, especially New York. We all cared so deeply and still do, for those whose lives were affected by the personal losses. Yet, we also knew we needed to continue to raise funds for the great charities our company represents.

The Rules of Fundraising changed in the weeks and months following 9/11. The question we all had to struggle with was, "How do we empathize with those so deserving of support while asking for funds for our own organization?" As fundraisers we adapted, as we always do, and found ways to honor the needs of others while appealing for funds for our own causes.

Here at Douglas Shaw & Associates we use a lot of "cover notes" or "lift-letters" as they're sometimes called because they lift response. We used these with both direct mail and income-producing newsletters. The cover notes acknowledged the current catastrophe, encouraged donors to help as they could and then tastefully drew them back to the ongoing work of the organizations we serve. This adaptation made for fantastic results!

Hurricane Katrina hit almost four years later, making landfall in Louisiana on August 29th. This time, we all saw it coming. Traveling about North America, as I do, people were seen glued to TV sets in airport and hotel restaurants and bars. The Weather Channel and The Weather Network probably had more viewers than at any other time in their histories!

Following this catastrophe, in spite of our best efforts, income was below forecast for many of the organizations we served in 2005. Even though we had been fully faithful to the rules and adapted where we could, the events surrounding Katrina were simply outside of our ability to overcome them. More money was contributed to Katrina relief than 9/11. Just about every youth group in the country held car washes, families spent their Thanksgivings building houses, churches made mission trips and donors gave generously. And I'm thrilled they did! Several years later the tsunami that devastated Japan and the massive earthquakes in Haiti grabbed the world's attention.

But because the media shifted more quickly to other stories and it didn't directly involve the American people, the negative impact on sustaining donations to nonprofits was minimal. Unfortunately, the good people of Haiti and Japan are still trying to put their lives and homes back together.

But catastrophic-level disasters still have a way of challenging the rules. However, for those organizations who are directly impacted by hurricanes, floods, fires and pestilence, the circumstances can also be a legitimate opportunity for raising much-needed income.

A few years ago, Memphis, Tennessee, was hit by a major summer storm. Electricity, water and other basic services were disrupted throughout Shelby County. We had planned a direct mail appeal for a homeless shelter there, and it was all sealed, stamped and ready to mail. A phone call from the president of the shelter prompted us to think carefully about what to do. "I can't send out a mailing that simply ignores what just happened," he said. We knew he was right. It was decided to review the content of the mailing for its appropriateness at a time like this; we decided that it certainly was appropriate since homeless people were being seriously impacted too.

We decided to place a large yellow label on the back side of the envelope with black printing on it that addressed the emergency situation and made the information inside all the more important. It performed well above our forecasted income! It is indeed true, sometimes the rules change.

RULE #33

"The rules of fundraising are sometimes applicable and sometimes not... that's why it can be helpful to have a guide."

To me, the Rules of Fundraising are a lot like learning Greek. When I was taking Greek in college and seminary one of the first things my professors taught me was that, in Greek, there is the rule, and then there are all the exceptions to the rule. This wasn't very comforting to me.

Like Greek, I have found that it helps to take fundraising rules in their context. There are, much to my dismay, many variables, and learning the variables can take an entire lifetime. Variables determine whether or not a specific rule is applicable.

Learning the variables of a situation makes a person more alert and valuable, traits worth pursuing for a fundraiser given the previously stated fact that the average lifespan of a director of development is only 18 months!

So what are the variables? Well...they vary!

I realize it can be confusing to learn that there are rules to fundraising and now you're being told there are times the rules don't apply. As an example of this, let's say one of the principles of snail-mail states: "You must have compelling copy (or teaser) on the outside of a direct mail envelope to get a donor or prospective donor to open it." Okay, that's easy enough to follow. But there are variables here that can make or break your best efforts.

VARIABLE #1:

"Compelling copy" means many things to many people. To be blunt, a fundraiser's opinion about what it means doesn't count. The only thing that matters here, as long as what's written is true, is whether or not it actually works, which means that the target audience takes the desired action of opening our letter.

VARIABLE #2:

Sometimes the most effective teaser is no teaser! A blank envelope can be the most compelling reason for a donor or a prospect to open an envelope. Their curiosity needs to be satisfied so they open it to find out who sent them a letter and why. It's a bit like an old faded road sign that can no longer be read. Does it say, "No Parking," or, I shudder at the thought, "No Fishing"? When I encounter one of these signs it bugs me the whole time that I'm away from my pickup doing my fly fishing thing. What does it say? What law am I supposed to be obeying? A blank envelope is kind of like this weather-worn sign. People have to know what's being said. So they open it, thinking maybe it's the credit card deal of the century or even an unexpected estate check from their distant uncle Louie.

VARIABLE #3:

Your compelling copy should not "spill the candy in the lobby"; i.e., it should not give away too much too soon, rather create, in the recipient, a desire to know more, which can only be satisfied by opening the direct mail package.

Many fundraisers make the mistake of giving away too much information on the outside of the envelope, making it unnecessary for the reader to open it.

VARIABLE #4:

There are many other variables! As I said, it will take a lifetime to learn all of the rules and variables. That's why some of us consultants still have jobs! Suffice it to say, it is critical to ask questions about what variables might apply to any of the Rules of Fundraising.

So you might approach the rules by asking something like this: "Okay, so this is the rule, now, does it always apply? Are there ever exceptions to this rule? What circumstances would cause this rule to be questioned?" As we've noted before, asking questions is critical in any situation. It's the assumptions we make that usually head us in the wrong direction.

Awhile back I took one of the most fascinating trips of my life. I flew to Alaska in the month of December to visit a potential client. To show me what their ministry was about, we flew 500 miles north and west from where they were stationed on the Kenai Peninsula, just south of Anchorage. Our trip took us through the magnificent snow-covered peaks, past Denali, which stood there in all its glory. Our flight was in a six-seat Navajo twin engine, and the weather conditions were perfect, so I had plenty of time to look around and snap a few pictures along the way.

We were headed to a small Inuit village about 90 miles southeast of Nome. We set down for fuel at a little airstrip that ran parallel to the Bering Sea. It was completely frozen over! The wind was blowing, and the actual temperature was 20 degrees below zero. After refueling, we climbed back into our little plane and set out on the last leg of our journey to the village of Golovin, a small spit of land jutting out into the frozen sea. We circled the village of about 200 inhabitants and then landed on a gravel strip between the inlet and the first row of houses in the village.

We spent the evening with a wonderful missionary couple and their little boy who had committed to living amongst the Inuit people. The next morning I awoke at about 7:00 AM. It was completely dark outside. When the sun began to rise, it wasn't in the east as I had assumed. At around 10:00 AM a small light began to appear to the south of us!

I tell you this story to illustrate this rule. Everyone knows the sun always rises in the east, except...when it's winter and you're near the Arctic Circle! Then it rises in the south and it sets in the south because the earth has tilted on its axis, and we were near the top of the world. What I witnessed during my first "day" in Golovin was five hours of a dimly lit sky during which the sun made a low arc on our southern horizon. By 3:00 PM it was totally dark again and the stars shined brightly overhead.

My assumptions about the sun have never been the same. Sometimes what we know to be true just isn't.

Experience is clearly the best teacher; but it also helps to travel with those who have seen the terrain before.

To summarize, "Sometimes the rules are applicable, and sometimes they're not." It requires knowledge and experience to recognize when situations with variables arise. Again, there are many friends in the philanthropic community, and we're all in this together. So don't be hesitant to ask a trusted colleague or consultant when you encounter something that looks like this rule of variables may apply.

RULE #34

"There are new rules being discovered every day."

Much of the thrill of fundraising comes in understanding that there are new rules being discovered every day. There's so much we have yet to learn about what motivates donors to give and abstain from giving.

With the seemingly daily breakthroughs occurring in technology, it's difficult to keep up with how to use them all. One thing we do know is that we need to use every tool in our box to communicate and fund our mission.

Hardly a day goes by that I don't read an article or hear a story about how an organization has found the secret to making significant income from social media. It reminds me of another technology from a long time ago...the telephone. When I was a kid, we had a game that we called "telephone." I don't know if this game is still being played in some form or another, but the idea was to have five or six people sit in a circle and one person begins with whispering a short statement into the ear of the person to the right of them. That person is supposed to whisper the exact same message to the person to their right, and the message continues all around the circle until the person who began the message says, "Alright, what did I say?" The last person to receive the whispered message would say what s/he heard. The message was never the same as the original. It had either been misunderstood or corrupted intentionally until it bore little resemblance to the beginning message. Upon announcing the permutated version, everybody would laugh and fall backward, howling and yelling.

Right now, stories about the use of social media for fundraising are being passed around the industry with much the same result as the game of "telephone." Whenever I dig deeper into the facts of the situation, I learn that what was purported to be $1,000,000 raised was indeed 1,000,000 likes on Facebook.

This process is nothing new. With the advent of radio, many media sages were predicting the immediate demise of the longstanding reign of newspapers, and television certainly was going to make radio unnecessary. After all, who would want to listen to the radio when they could watch television? The same kind of thinking continues today. The Internet has replaced everything, or has it?

There is certainly a massive segmentation of media occurring. And yes, newspapers are not doing very well these days. But to predict the demise or success of one form of media over all others doesn't have history on its side.

There is no questioning the impact of social media on our daily lives. In fact, one of my children married a person they met through a popular online service. Years ago my answer appalled people who would ask me how my children met their significant others. Today these same people wouldn't even blink.

Online fundraising is increasing in its effectiveness as people become more comfortable with using their credit cards to make donations and purchases. But as I've mentioned earlier, here in the U.S., online donations now account for about 30% of all giving.

The rules for digital media are still being formed. But there is no question that digital media is a valid and essential income and engagement source that cannot be overlooked. Even as we grapple to identify the rules for this media, new media is being developed, and new rules will certainly emerge.

The 35 rules articulated here are just those that my colleagues and I are able to recognize and articulate as of now. Give us a couple more days, and we'll think of a few more. In fact, now that I think about it, just two days ago I learned about The Rule of Threes. This is a great little rule. It helps me to understand why there are times when some of the rules don't work.

The Rule of Threes states the following: "If you've just had three very productive fundraising snail-mail appeals in a row, the fourth and fifth appeals, no matter how closely you've followed the rules, will not perform at optimum levels."

Not encouraging news, I realize. It's kind of like hearing, you have a head cold but you'll be feeling better in 7-10 days! Or perhaps more realistically, it's like hearing that the only way to really lose weight is through diet and exercise! I lend my voice to all of the others who've said, "Why can't they just invent a pill!" But, alas, no pill exists regardless of what they say on late night television...but there is Ozempic!

If we think about it, donors who have responded generously for three appeals in a row may decide it's time to take a bit of a breather. This rule may come from something as simple as this.

But it's better that you know this rule so you can keep it in your hip pocket and use it when you need to, like during forecasting for your upcoming budget. Besides, when giving doesn't meet your forecast, it sounds much more sophisticated than, "I think it's the economy!"

RULE #35

"You will have times when you succeed, and you will have times when you fail, miserably."

I distinctly remember when I was just entering my thirties and I wanted to do everything within my power to learn from everybody else's mistakes. You see, I didn't want to make any significant mistakes of my own. The way I figured it, if I could just read about the mistakes of others, listen to the other poor saps who'd stumbled their way through life to emerge with their self-esteem partially intact and watch everyone around me with any experience, I could come through life relatively unscathed. Oh, silly me! But at the time it didn't feel silly at all.

Perfection wasn't my intended goal. I had, by this time in my life, thankfully lost this illusion. I knew I wasn't better than anybody else, and was probably worse than many. So it wasn't about wanting to achieve world peace or anything. My fixation with mistakes was largely focused on my desire to make a difference in the world while being seen as competent enough to make a living.

Now, I've never felt that I have been naturally gifted at anything. Nothing in sports, music or education ever changed my opinion about this. In fact, everything, up to this time, had confirmed my lack of being a "natural." I think this is why I was so fixated on becoming a great fundraiser; I just desperately wanted and needed to be good at something!

As I mentioned in the introduction to this book, after graduate school, an opportunity arose to help poor people throughout the world. I secured a position at a relief and development organization. An opportunity opened up within the ministry to apply for a development position, so I decided to become a professional fundraiser! Progress didn't come overnight. I wasn't a "natural" at fundraising either. In fact, I now began to question the whole concept of someone being a natural. It seemed to me that drive, determination and insatiable curiosity were more desirable traits.

I decided I would become a dedicated student of direct response marketing and fundraising. I read books, attended seminars and talked to all the knowledgeable people in the industry who'd spend time with me. In short, I began asking questions rather than making assumptions. I found the asking of questions to be the key to my understanding.

By age 30, I knew I was making mistakes at every turn, but a fundraising firm decided to hire me anyway. They must have seen something in me that made me worth hiring. I had, after all, spent three years working in development for a nonprofit.

I began my agency life largely executing the strategies provided to me by more experienced consultants. Over time I learned some of the rules of our craft, moved slightly beyond the point of being dangerous and began to enjoy some success.

After several years, I was named vice president for client services and managed about $10,000,000 in accounts, about a third of the agency's business. I had hit my share of potholes along the way and was learning to recover from them about as much as anybody can. But then I did something pretty risky. A trusted client asked me to help them raise money on the radio in Los Angeles. It was pretty heady stuff, negotiating with radio stations and telephone call centers and planning a radiothon in the media capital of the world. The only problem was, at the time, I didn't know the rules about raising money on the air. The day of the broadcast the phones weren't ringing as I was sure they would.

Needless to say, I began to have a sinking feeling after about two hours in. We still had six hours to go, and I didn't know what to do. I began scratching my thinning hair. I had outrun my experience, and there was no one to blame but myself. My client was working hard, telling the stories of how homeless people had been helped through his rescue mission. Former homeless men and women were ushered in and out of the studio, telling their stories of changed lives. Celebrities were sitting in, giving their endorsements and asking people to call. And a few did. But all in all, it was a miserable failure. We had spent far more than we raised, and I was the culprit. It was a difficult drive back to my hotel that night and a very long flight back home from L.A.

Thankfully I had a strong track record of success with my client and an excellent relationship. He never even lectured me or mentioned the radiothon again. I continued to serve the organization for several years, remaining carefully in my areas of expertise while vowing to learn how to raise money through radio.

After 12 years working in four different fundraising agencies, my skills were still improving; in fact, I was beginning to behave as a consultant should. My assigned clients were raising money, and I was building solid relationships within the marketplace. I continued to seek to discover the Rules of Fundraising with an unsurpassed appetite.

By the summer of 1994, when I was working in my fourth agency and had moved my family several times, I was well on my way to becoming a journeyman fundraiser. My work was gaining in reputation to the point that clients began asking me, "Why don't you open your own firm, Doug? If you did, I'd hire you!"

The thought of owning my own fundraising firm had been in my thinking for some time. I had an increasing desire to shape the culture and values of my own shop. My work in multiple agencies had taught me much about what to do and, perhaps more importantly, what not to do.

On October 24th of 1994, Douglas Shaw & Associates was born. My family and I decided to relocate back to Wheaton, Illinois, where we could raise our children in a community we had once lived. The Chicago area was also a great place for business, had two airports and there were no significant competing agencies there that were serving our market.

We started our little business in the basement of our home on Washington Street. Within three years we found it awkward to have employees raiding our refrigerator and decided it was time to move into a "real office."

Today, our firm occupies 15,000 square feet in an office building in Naperville, Illinois. Douglas Shaw & Associates serves more than 30 clients ranging from local rescue missions to well-known national and international ministries and organizations.

Our staff of 65 amazes me every day with their heart, brilliance and sense of determination to serve high impact nonprofits. I am still CEO in our company and have enjoyed watching our company grow and serve. We have made countless mistakes and will make many more. I no longer have the illusion of merely learning from other's mistakes. I've had to come to grips with the reality that learning the Rules of Fundraising and profiting from "the yeast of failure" are the best mentors. Providing fundraising consulting to what I consider God's work in this world is exceedingly fulfilling, and I hope this book serves you well in your own journey through the successes and failures of your own career.

CONCLUSION

As we began our journey, I expressed my desire for you to see The Rules of Fundraising for what they really are—a helpful set of tools to encourage you, clear the path ahead of you and give you a craftsman's confidence as you use them in raising funds for your philanthropic cause.

I'd like to think of you sitting in your workshop carefully crafting your ideas, with colleagues running in and out making certain the execution of your plans are being carefully shaped by your mind, heart and hand.

Along the way I've spun a few stories hoping to provide substance and practical examples and to illustrate the best practices of fundraising in a memorable fashion. My main, underlying purpose was to provide you with a toolbox to reach into whenever you desire to sharpen your skills, find a new tool when you need one and provide you with the implements that are familiar to your hand.

My goal has been to help you comprehend that there are indeed rules involved in fundraising. Again, these are not my rules. They are bodies of knowledge known to those who have successfully labored in the fields of philanthropy for decades.

Even though we don't get to make them, we can begin to search for them like the nuggets of gold they are. Their great value comes from the fact that they are rare knowledge.

Learn them and you will greatly enhance your skill and your ability to provide the valuable resources that your nonprofit so dearly needs.

In no way are these rules a comprehensive compilation. But now that you know to look for them, you too can contribute to the great body of knowledge that drives successful fundraising.

It's my ultimate goal, however, to give you the gift of hope that has been so generously shared with me by the many journeymen and master craftsmen of our trade. After all, we all need each other in this great profession of philanthropic encouragement. Because there's an entire world out there, filled with needs that only the Lord can meet, and he is choosing to do some of it through the exercising of your special craft.

Embrace the journey, discover new rules, use them to soar and articulate them to the rest of us who need all the assistance we can gather to make our needy world a place of hope for those who hurt; a place of fulfillment for those who are hungry for everything that's good. May you have peace and joy on your journey, and may God grant you the wisdom to know that you are not alone and help is nearby.

BIBLIOGRAPHY

Berton, P. (1984). *The Promised Land: Settling the West 1896-1814*. Anchor Canada, a division of Random House of Canada Ltd.

Gelb, M. & Caldicott, S. M. (2007). *Innovate Like Edison: The Success System of America's Greatest Inventor.* New York: Penguin Group (USA) Inc.

Stanley, T. J. & Danko, W.D. (1996). *The Millionaire Next Door: The Surprising Secrets of America's Wealthy*. New York: Pocket Books.

DePree, M. (1990). *Leadership is an Art.* New York, NY: Doubleday.

DePree, M. (1992). *Leadership Jazz*. New York: Dell Publishing.

Greenleaf, R. K. (1977). *Servant Leadership: A Journey into the Nature of Legitimate Power and Greatness.* New York: Paulist Press.

Lutzer, E. W. (1997). *One Minute After You Die.* Chicago: Moody Publishers.

Geever, J. C. (1997). *The Foundation Center's Guide to Proposal Writing.* The Foundation Center.

Nouwen, H. J. (2010). *The Henri Nouwen Spirituality Series: A Spirituality of Fundraising.* The Henri Nouwen Legacy Trust.

Panas, J. (1984). *Mega Gifts: Who Gives Them, Who Gets Them.* Chicago: Pluribus Press, Inc.

Sturtevant, W. T. (2004). *The Artful Journey: Cultivating and Soliciting The Major Gift.* Chicago: Institutions Press.

Sturtevant, W. T. (2001). *The Continuing Journey: Stewardship and Useful Case Studies in Philanthropy.* Chicago: Bonus Books, Inc.

Trout, J., & Ries, A. (1981, 1986). *Positioning: The Battle for Your Mind.* McGraw-Hill, Inc.

Warwick, M. (2004). *Revolution in the Mailbox: Your Guide to Successful Direct Mail Fundraising*. San Francisco, CA, United States: Jossey-Bass.

The Institute for Charitable Giving
500 North Michigan Avenue, Suite 2008
Chicago, Illinois 60611
phone: (800) 234-7777 | *www.instituteforgiving.org*
Mark Twain quotations - Adam
www.twainquotes.com/Adam.html

ABOUT THE AUTHOR

DOUGLAS K. SHAW

Douglas K. Shaw has been the Chairman/CEO of Douglas Shaw & Associates, a leading direct response fundraising firm, for 31 years. During his 45-year career, he has consulted with hundreds of high-impact leaders and companies. His firm raises hundreds of millions of dollars annually for nonprofit organizations and ministries that change the lives of men, women, and children.

Doug holds a Bachelor of Arts degree in History from Simpson University and a Master of Arts degree in Theology from Fuller Seminary. He is the author of three other books: *Curative Culture*, *More Rules of Fundraising*, and *The Six Essentials of Rapidly Growing Nonprofits*. Doug resides in his home state of Washington, where he and his wife Kathryn enjoy entertaining family and friends while exploring the wonders of creation.

DON'T MISS THESE OTHER BOOKS BY DOUGLAS K. SHAW

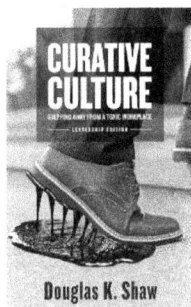

CURATIVE CULTURE: STEPPING AWAY FROM A TOXIC WORKPLACE

Curative Culture offers real-world examples for leaders who want to step away from a toxic environment, build a more profitable business, and achieve excellence. Through thoughtful stories and practical insight, Shaw invites leaders and teams to imagine a better way of working – rooted in trust, dignity, and shared humanity.

MORE RULES OF FUNDRAISING

More Rules of Fundraising—a continuation of *The Rules of Fundraising*—provides 35 additional rules, never before written down, that must be used in order to be a success in your fundraising efforts.

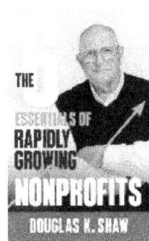

THE SIX ESSENTIALS OF RAPIDLY GROWING NONPROFITS

What are the common traits all rapidly growing nonprofits share? *The Six Essentials of Rapidly Growing Nonprofits* holds the answers to this oft-asked question! A must read for everyone who serves by working in a nonprofit organization, including board members, CEOs, and Development Officers.

ORDER YOUR COPY TODAY!

Scan this QR code to order your copy of these fundraising resources.

www.ingramcontent.com/pod-product-compliance
Lightning Source LLC
Chambersburg PA
CBHW071340210328
41597CB00015B/1517